WomanStrength:
Modern Church, Modern Women

Sr. Joan Chittister, O.S.B.

Sheed & Ward

Acknowledgements

The Publisher gratefully acknowledges permission to reprint the following materials: "Woman: Icon, Rebel, Saint" appeared in *The Grail* (Vol. 4); "Of Moses' Mother and Pharaoh's Daughter: A Model of Contemporary Contemplation" appeared in *The Merton Annual III*; "Formation for Ministry" was published in *The Way* (No. 62); "Peace is Worth Getting Riled About" and "The Spirituality of St. Benedict" are reprinted from *U.S. Catholic* (Vol. 54); "A Rule of Life," a three-part interview, is reprinted from *Sojourners* (Vol. 16).

Sheed & Ward™ is a service of National Catholic Reporter Publishing Company, Inc.

Library of Congress Catalog Card Number: 90-61956

ISBN: 1-55612-373-6

Published by: Sheed & Ward
115 E. Armour Blvd. P.O. Box 419492
Kansas City, MO 64141

To order, call: (800) 333-7373

Contents

1

WomanStrength

The question of the role of women in church and society has been a long-standing tug-of-war and is yet to be clearly, universally and unequivocally resolved. In some situations, the attitude is obviously "Ah, the ladies, God bless 'em," and in other situations—even in nice company—it's clearly "Oh, the women, God help us." The track record is at best ambiguous and clearly long-standing: "No trust is to be placed in women," Homer wrote centuries before Christ (*Odyssey*, XI). "It is thy place, woman, to hold thy peace and keep within doors," Aeschylus said (*The Seven Against Thebes*). "Woman is an inferior man," Aristotle decided (*Poetics*, XV). George Herbert taught in the 17th century, "Take heed of a young wench, a prophetess, and a Latin-bred woman," (*Jacula Prudentam,* 1651) which does not, obviously, leave room for much in the way of women besides the dumb, the quiet and the docile. And Schopenhauer declared in the 19th century, "A woman represents a sort of intermediate stage between a child and a man," (*Parerge und Paralipomena*).

May Sarton, on the other hand, said, "Woman's work is always toward wholeness." And Louise Nevelson wrote, "The freer that women become, the freer men will be, because when you enslave another, you have enslaved yourself." Elizabeth Cady Stanton warned us, "Woman's discontent increases in exact proportion to her development," and George Eliot said, "I'm not denying that women are foolish. After all, God almighty made them to match the men." Finally, Louisa May Alcott wrote, "Women have been called queens for a long time, but the kingdom that they give them to rule isn't worth the ruling."

Clearly, there are two views about the role and place of women in the world. And the problem is, why? There is one question, I

1

think, that races underground in the human psyche, too obvious to deserve an answer, but too eternally present to be ignored. The world debates one set of questions—the ones for which answers come easy or, if they come hard, come at least with a passionate commitment. But under them all in the deepest recesses of history and mythology and anthropology lies the fundamental question that must someday, finally, once-and-for-all be faced. And that question is not "Should women and men receive equal pay for equal work?" That question is not, "Should women be ordained?" That question is not, "Should women be both represented and representatives?" That question is not "Should women be free from the ownership of men and the control of men and the physical brutality of men?"

No, those questions are the simple ones. The answers to those questions, once you really accept the answer to the first question, the central question, the underlying question, can only be yes: yes to equal wages, yes to ordination, yes to self-sufficiency, yes to intellectual development, yes to truth and independence and voice. Yes. Yes. Yes.

Then why don't we get unmitigated, unmodified, unamended yeses from the governments and the corporations and the Church? Why don't the laws show yes and the senates show yes? And the seminaries show yes and the synods show yes? We don't get yes yet, I argue, because male governments and corporations and churches—now as always and always as now—are not really convinced of the truth of the unspoken, the bedrock question, the question that is always timely and wearyingly timeless. Indeed, the actual question is simply, "Are women really human beings or not?"

People who will not insist that a 21-year old man needs protection and direction will assume that a 21-year old "girl" does. People who would never question the sanity of a soldier spraying napalm on old men and small children will routinely question the emotional stability of menstruating women. People who would never assume that a woman needs money of her own take for granted that a man does. And why? Because when men across the centuries—school men, church men, men of science, men of law—have asked whether or not women were whole beings—whole in mind, whole in body, whole in soul, the answer has seldom, if ever, been yes.

When men decided that women's birthing powers unleashed havoc on the world and, therefore, women would need to be controlled by men, their answer was clearly that women had human bodies but only half the human soul. When Plato and Aristotle and Thomas Aquinas decided that women were emotionally unstable and intellectually inferior, the answer certainly was that women had services to give but no necessarily human ideas to develop. When women were kept by law—both church law and civil law— off the streets and out of the universities and in the kitchens and away from the churches, when women were put in sole charge of services to children and comforts to men but never of adult concerns, the answer was undoubtedly that women were minors grown large but not persons grown up. When they defined the sacramental system, men decided that women could get some graces but not all graces, that they could get grace, but they could never give it, that God had apparently made pink and blue souls and that, undoubtedly, the pink ones leak. And, oh, the message is so clear.

I know a woman in Haiti who walks four hours a day for water because carrying water is women's work, and the government won't pay money to lay water pipes when they have women pack animals that can do the same work for nothing. I know women in Mexico whose husbands beat them for attending meetings at the women's co-op because the men believe that meetings of women are a useless waste of time that should be spent instead on them. I know a widow in Erie, Pennsylvania who lives on a pittance, on less than $300 a month, because her husband died before retirement and widows do not receive the man's entire Social Security check—only part of it—despite the fact that it is men who have decreed that women belong in the home. I know women in the Philippines who take their children to the garbage cans of the city at 4:00 A.M. each night to scavenge for the next day's dinner because that's when the restaurants of the city put their garbage out and because men claim the overcrowded lean-tos for sleep at night and leave the women to find an hour or two of rest in the middle of their chaotic days. I know a woman who has wrestled all her life—since she was six years old, in fact—with the incest that male moralists have decreed is the woman's fault, unless, of course, she is willing to resist to death rather than live with what men call the dishonor of having been raped. I know a woman with an M. Div. degree from an accredited Roman Catholic seminary who wears herself out day in and day out, caring for people, listening to their pain, developing their liturgies, teaching their children catechism, while men say that her ministry to the church, in the church, is not "official."

Indeed, when women are left out of cabinets and councils and corporate boards and chanceries, when women are beaten in the United States and sold for bride-price in India and denied access to farm equipment in Africa and cast out for not bearing sons in Arabia and sold into prostitution in the Philippines and exposed as infants on the dung heaps of China and used, abused and abandoned in Central America, the answer is very, very clear. As far as men are concerned, the answer is that women are half-souled, half-graced, and half-human—and the answer is wrong.

There is in woman what this world lacks and sorely needs and is groaning without. There is in woman the potential for the preservation of the globe, the health of society and the community life of the human race. And how can we possibly know that? And where can we go to see it? And what can it possibly mean to us today? Ironically enough, what men have taught to keep women in their place is exactly what demands that they be raised up.

Women are different than men, the philosophers taught. Exactly! So let's hear from them. Women are created from Adam, "bone of my bone . . . flesh of my flesh," the churchmen taught. If you say so—but then, the two must be intellectual—and spiritual—equals, right? If for no other reason than the DNA! Women have a special role in the creation and the development of life, the doctors taught. Absolutely—so why do we put the preservation of the planet solely in the hands of men when the preservation of the planet is so desperately at stake? "In God's image God made them; male and female God made them," Scripture says. All of life depends on the balance of the *anima*—the feminine—and the *animus* or masculine, Jungian psychology says.

Nevertheless, the world and the Church are both guided only by the masculine half, by masculine means, for masculine meanings alone. And as a result, the world walks on one leg and sees with one eye and thinks with only one-half of the human brain—and it shows. We have only half a human rights policy in this world, and only half our needs are being met. And half our human vision—the half that cares about hunger and poverty and homelessness and equality—is missing. In the U.S. budget of 1986, $0.64 of every disposable dollar went for military expenses, past or present, and $0.20 went for all the human services—health, education, housing, welfare—combined, all of them the concerns mainly of women and children, about whom every male politician talks and to whom none of them listen. Indeed, the world needs a feminine presence, a feminine perspective, a feminine process for dealing with problems, a feminine perception of what is true and what is necessary and what is valuable.

Indeed, the world needs more now than tokenism. Tokenism, of course, is a strategy that lies in letting one of the underclass in—a minority here, a minority there—middle management maybe, but nothing serious—in order to keep the rest of an out-group out and look good at the same time. Tokenism is one woman in a space craft, one woman on the board, one woman in the department, one woman on the bishop's staff. No, tokenism is definitely not equality. Tokenism changes nothing. The system stays male—only the letterhead and the pictures on the PR brochures change. Tokenism simply brings the dissonance into the board room in order to ignore it or outvote it or persuade it. Tokenism, in fact, takes special care to see that power and place are definitely not shared, and that the dominant still dominate.

Three women in a crew of six in a spacecraft would be equality. Ten women on a board of twenty would be equality. Fifty female seminarians out of a class of one hundred would be equality. The joint ordination of married deacons and deaconesses—now that would be equality. And it is equality that we need. And why? Because women are human and because half of humanity is missing from the very centers of life and because life itself is suffering from a system skewed and sickened by male myopia and paralysis and social lobotomy.

But what would women bring to a Church in crisis and a planet in peril? Women would bring woman, that's what women would bring. And it is woman that is the invisible gift, the unseen presence, the gaping shadow on the world horizon. We talk only about him, we elect only him, we ordain only him, we promote only him. We make him the norm and the judge and the power in and of and over all of humankind.

It is indeed woman that women must bring—the missing dimension of human life, the lost art of human beauty, the final arbiter of the true quality of human justice. "The basic discovery about any people is the discovery of the relationship between its men and women," Pearl Buck wrote. Well, by those standards, to discover the world in which we live is to discover it deficient. At the same time, the American poet Muriel Rukeyser said, "The universe is made of stories, not of atoms." And women have stories aplenty of what it is to hold the universe together a woman's way.

The feminine dimension of life, Jung teaches, lies in intuition, flexibility, self-sacrifice, receptivity, support, and feeling. And every one of those qualities have been used against women to keep women in psychological bondage. But every one of them, too, is a gift, sadly lacking and sorely needed in this for-males-only world. But the stories of women and models of women alive and gifting have touched every age and surround us even now and give us hope and drive us on.

Who are the women of the past and the present, then, whose gifts of intuition and flexibility, self-sacrifice and receptivity, support and feeling have made the kind of difference that we need now? Who are the women that God has raised up to show us what women can do, and where are the women who are giving, giving, giving—despite opposition and rejection and disdain—the saving gifts of women yet? And what do they say to us? From the revelation of Scripture to the reports on the daily news, their numbers and their names are legion, though they have been seldom recognized and rarely affirmed.

Intuition is feminine and order is masculine, Jung taught. Well, Moses' mother had an intuition that no woman could see the face of the oppressed and oppress it. With great faith and keen insight, she set her condemned Jewish infant where the daughter of the Egyptian king herself would find this doomed child, and together the Jewish woman and the Arab woman joined hands across their differences to subvert the enemy system that male order and reason had devised. And due to woman's intuition and creativity and passion for life, an entire people was saved. In Argentina, in our time too, the mothers of the Plaza de Mayo had an intuition that no oppressor could forever withstand the shrill, strong voice of truth. And day after day after day, they wept aloud for all the world to see. And the government fell. And the people were saved by the intuitive strength of old women who refused to accept what order and "logic" had decreed.

Indeed, intuition is the woman's gift that is meant to balance the male passion for order without heart. Flexibility is feminine and control is masculine, the psychologists tell us. And the woman of God, Ruth, knew the strength that came with flexibility. Ruth could, when truth and integrity demanded it, change her ideas and change her allegiances and change her very life. And Ruth saw a value seen by few. Ruth saw the value in another woman and laid down her life for it. When Naomi, her mother-in-law, an outcast widow, a hated foreigner, a Moabite, urged Ruth to go her own way in a culture that rejected the feminine, attached its women to men and despised its useless widows, Ruth changed her world view about the law and the customs and the right way of doing things to embrace a bolder vision. She pledged herself, instead, to take care of the woman her society called worthless and outcast. So much for male control and its penchant for traditions and prescriptions and certainties made by men, primarily for their own good.

Flexibility is without doubt, in a time of organized enmity and intransigent world views, a woman's strength and a universal need. In our time, too, in Israel, the Jewish women in black go every day to the Wailing Wall rigid with tradition and pray the prayers that for centuries only men have prayed there. The pious Jewish men, of course, beat them for it: these women have, the men will tell you—heatedly righteous—transgressed the will of God. There is no report, on the other hand, that God has apparently beaten them at all. Indeed, male rigidity is carving up the world into armed camps to destroy it. At a time when the male characteristic of control has been found counterfeit, clearly the world needs the feminine flexibility of Naomi and the women in black if it is to be saved at all.

Self-sacrifice is a feminine quality, Jung taught, that is necessary in a world devoted to the masculine values of profit and gain. Indeed, we have been well taught. In this society, it is truly every man for himself and winning by intimidation. But the fact is that, as a result, few are really winning at all. Queen Esther is the woman God lifted up to model the power of feminine self-sacrifice. Esther is Scripture's well-placed woman who has no experience of suffering, no threat of death, no fear of loss of place. Esther is safe and respected and affirmed. Esther is a "lady" who knows her place in a world where self-development is a male prerogative. But Esther is willing for the sake of her people to sacrifice it all, her position, her security, her very life. "I will go to the king to plead for the people," Esther says, "whether he calls me or not. And if I perish, I perish." And on her account, the people thrived. Surely the world needs self-sacrifice now. When men are trained simply to take orders without question, when the best rock no boats, call no consciences, critique no systems for fear of falling off the corporate or ecclesiastical ladder, then someone must be willing to die for the truth or the ovens in Auschwitz, the killing fields in My Lai, the arms deals in Washington, and the churches where Jesus says to women, "Don't follow me," will continue to wring the life out of life.

In our own time, in Nicaragua, the Sisters of St. Agnes have been working with the Miskito Indians for 45 years, doing what nuns do: teaching catechism, tutoring children, caring for the poor . . . being safe and respected and secure—being "good sisters," quiet and docile and invisible. Until a few years ago when they began to see the people driven off their lands, destroyed in their beds, diminished as a people for generations to come. Then they threw caution to the wind, and began to accompany the Meskito Indians back to their ancestral lands in the Bluefields region—back past the army, back past the government observers, back past the angry war zones where self-sacrifice claimed the life last month of two of their sisters and maimed two others. But where the narcissism of machoism cannot succeed because of it. And where a whole people have new life as a result.

Receptivity is feminine and aggression is masculine, we're taught. And receptivity, the masculine world says, is weakness. But receptivity is all we have between us and the other. Receptivity is the only answer we have to the enemy "impossibility" that lurks within us. The woman of God, Sarah, was receptive to the possibility that what seemed natural was not necessary. "Sarah will conceive in her old age," the angel told Abraham. And, the Scripture says, "Sarah laughed." But I don't think Sarah laughed, I think Sarah hooted. She was way past menopause. Way past child-bearing age. Way past the very thought of pregnancy. And she told the angel so. But when the impossible happened, she was open to it. She didn't reject it; she didn't resist it. She didn't demand her own way. She didn't set out to wrench the world to her own design. Receptivity is the quality which, as Mark Van Doren says, "Takes ideas in and treats them royally, on the grounds that someday one of them may be king." Today in Northern Ireland, Catholic women who call themselves "Peace People" have reached out with warmth and love to embrace the impossible idea that Protestants and Catholics can bridge the chasm that inflexible religious barriers have created and together heal the wounds that closed-mindedness and aggression have caused. Here, acceptance rather than aggression has healed more of the horrors of war than soldiers or politicians have been able to allay in all the time of national tension before and after them. Thanks to the flexibility of these women, the world knows that ecumenism is real and peace between opposites is possible.

The world knows, too, then, that the strong, masculine domination that we have idolized has failed us. Jung says that support is a feminine characteristic and competition is male. This society, of course, prides itself that it is built on competition. But competition makes enemies of what could and should be friends. It is support, on the other hand, that holds the world together. It is support that makes the impossible possible and the unattainable reachable and the difficult doable. It is the support of the Samaritan woman, the one who is the wrong religion and the wrong lifestyle and the wrong sex, that brings Jesus first to the non-Jew. It is the Samaritan woman who is the prophet's prophet, who speaks where Jesus cannot as Moses did for Aaron. It is the Samaritan woman who sees and hears and believes and preaches when all the professional believers are competing to be right and be first and be in charge. And it is still support that the world needs.

Everyday the government throws more guns into the "war" against drugs and invades countries to stop there what we cannot apparently stop here. But the corruption and the killings go on. In Detroit, one woman, Clementine Chism Barfield, whose own teenage sons—aged 15 and 16—were shot to death by teenage gangs, has stepped forward to bring support to children struggling with the drug culture. SOSAD—Save our Sons and Daughters—is credited by police officials in the city with helping to reduce youth homicide in Detroit by 25%, not because she went into the situation with muscle and force but because she went with love and care, with vision and gentleness, with sensitivity and support—because, in other words, she went into this public issue a woman's way.

Jung says that feeling is a feminine characteristic and reason is male. The male world also says that it is feeling that really enfeebles a woman. High Vatican officials have recently issued warnings about the presence of women on marriage tribunals, in fact, because

". . . their tender hearts render them unable to make right judgments . . ."—as if women weren't the other half of the marriage system. Feeling corrodes the brain, in other words. Feelings weaken the will. Feelings obscure the truth. A grand Church doctrine, apparently, and taught in the name of God, of course. Well, tell that to the Mary who washed the feet of Jesus with her tears and dried them with her hair. Tell that to the Marys who followed Jesus all the way to the cross. Tell that to the Mary who went "weeping to the tomb." Who even remembers and above all, who cares about all the "reasonable" men who were not with the women in those places where all the world has since wanted to be? Oh, yes, tell the women who recognized Jesus for the rest of us that feeling is their downfall and our bane and the disease that renders women unfit for human service. In fact, tell all the women of the world that feeling is unreasonable and unbearable and unvaluable and unimportant to the development of peoples and the preservation of the planet.

Tell the women in India, who feel that wife burnings and dowry demands and the abortion of female fetuses must stop, that their feelings have enfeebled their minds. Tell the women in Africa, who feel that the excision of female genitalia to control a woman's sexual responses and assure her fidelity must stop, that their feelings have enfeebled their minds. Tell the women in Central America, who are beginning co-ops and literacy programs because they feel that economic dependence is simply another form of slavery, that they must stop their organizing of women because their feelings are enfeebling their minds. Tell my women friends in the Philippines, who have been raped because they are against rape, that their feelings and their faith in the full humanity of women must stop. Tell all the women's groups in the United States and throughout the world that they must stop caring when the world is only half-free, half-whole, half-feeling and half-human.

The fact is that the male characterisitics of order and logic, control and competition, aggression and reason and independence have often betrayed us and led us astray and left us bereft of the best, the real best in life. The fact is that the unilateral and universal male track record, as I read it, is division and invasion and rape and plunder and holocaust and depression and starvation and war and the planned destruction of humankind and now the very deterioration of the planet. I am not arguing that women will necessarily do better. I am simply saying that it would be impossible for them to do worse.

So what is the question before the human race, the response to which may well decide the future of life on earth? And what is the answer? The question is surely, "Is thinking a woman's work?" And the answer is certainly, "Are women human?" The question is, "Should women be in decision-making positions?" And the answer must be, "Are women human?" The question is, "Do women have anything to contribute to international relations and ecology and peace and human development?" And the answer must be, "Are women human?" The question certainly is, "Can the Church possibly be whole without women?" And the answer without doubt is, "Are women human?" It is time to answer the real question, the basic question, the fundamental question. "Are women really human beings or not?" When we answer that question, all the other answers follow automatically, immediately, clearly.

You see, it is not what sexism says about women that is sinful. It is what sexism says about God that is heresy. Doesn't sexism really imply that God is all powerful—except when it comes to women, at which point the God who could draw water from a rock and raise the dead to life is totally powerless to work as fully through a woman as through a man? This same God who also said, "Let us make humans in our own image, female and male let us make them." What will women bring to a Church in crisis and a planet in peril? Women will bring woman, that's what! And women will bring the feminine intuition that senses crisis and responds to it creatively; the flexibility that recognizes the value of another way of doing things; the self-sacrifice that cares for the other and the everyone and the earth to the equal good of all; the receptivity that makes enemies friends; the support that makes the difficult possible and the uncertain sure and division deplorable; the feeling that bonds differences and binds people together and makes equality a strength rather than a fear. Most of all, in our day, women will bring intuition and flexibility, self-sacrifice and receptivity, feeling and support to a world that is drowning in unreasonable reasoning and disordered logic and corrupting control and angry aggression and selfish competition and sinful independence and the idolatry of maleness writ anew while the earth wilts and the peoples starve. And the sacraments daily, daily disappear. What the world needs now if the world is, indeed, to survive is cooperation, not control, consensus instead of competition, collaboration rather than coercion. What the world needs now is woman.

Camus has said that the saints of our time are those who refuse to be either its executioners or its victims. We know, of course, that nothing we do changes the past. But we must realize that everything we do changes the future.

I'm begging you for the sake of the children, for the sake of the Church, for the sake of the people, for the sake of the planet to refuse to be either the executioner or the victim. Do something to lead the world to receive, to accept, to recognize the missing, the necessary, the phenomenal gift of woman.

2

Sexism in the Church: Agenda for the Next Decade

There are two stories, perhaps, which indicate with greatest precision the purpose and the power of a gathering of people that comes together from everywhere and from nowhere in particular, one at a time, and together, to consider the unfulfilled promise of the creation of women that daily, daily, nags for resolution.

The first story is from the life of Margaret Mead.

They asked the great anthropologist, "Doctor Mead, what are the most important periods of human development in all of history?" And, it is said, Margaret Mead responded without hesitation: "There are four periods in human history," she explained, "after which nothing was ever again the same—and those times are the period of evolution; the period of the ice age; the age of industrialization; and the period of the women's movement."

The other story is much older—and much more demanding.

Among the religious literature of the ancient East comes this other insight: A woman, whose whole struggle in life had been the unrealized search for full human development, complained to the holy one that, despite herself, destiny made the personal fulfillment for which she sought so sincerely unachievable. And the holy one said, "But that is impossible. It is you who make your destiny." But the woman protested, "Surely you are not saying, holy one, that I am responsible for being born a woman?" And the holy one answered: "You don't understand. Being born a woman is not destiny. Being born a woman is fate. Destiny," the seer said, "is how you accept that womanhood and destiny is what you make of it."

14

The messages and meanings are clear. In the first place, the women's movement is a growing, swelling, ongoing, cultural current of social change. And secondly, it is all up to us. The prophetic power of transformation of the face of the Church, no, of the world, is with us today. And, God knows, the world is in need of transformation. Things simply must not go on as they have been and still are now for women: unwhole, unhealthy, unrepentant, and unfulfilled, but the real problem is that whether things go on for women in the future as they have in the past depends on what you and I do with things as they are.

What, indeed, must be our own agenda for the 90s? And, most of all, where do we get it? And how shall we recognize it when we see it? And how shall we distinguish between the false gods and the true in a movement called alternately both good and evil? How shall we know that we are being good church as well as good feminists?

There are signs in the culture, of course. The oppression of women has finally run out of scientific steam. What was once scientifically posited simply cannot be scientifically proven. There is no scientific proof whatsoever to the old philosophical truism that women—as a class—are inferior to men as a class. It's just not true, the research confirms, that women are less intelligent, or less emotionally stable, or less physically capable, or less biologically complete, or less socially equipped, or less spiritually insightful than men. The Maccoby studies confirm the fact that women are just as bright—or brighter—than male students, all the way to college. Then, the Horner research shows us, young women begin to fear that being too bright will bring them social disapproval, will make them less marriageable, and so, the young women deliberately begin to limit their academic performance—or, at least, to do the fellow's homework.

What was once explained, in other words, as a spurt of development for men is really a curb on development by women. According to NASA, space travel research indicates that pound for pound, inch for inch, muscle for muscle, women show more physical endurance than men. Biological analyses reveal that the aging process—the human deterioration problem—is a function of the male hormone, not the female hormone.

The Smith-Rosenberg studies, in their critique of the Freudian hysteria data, uncovered the fact that the one emotional factor common to each of Freud's women patients was not their envy of men. It was their rage at having been dismissed themselves as ineffective because they were women.

The Broverman work in mental health research contends that the most mentally healthy people are androgenous people—people who have fully developed both the masculine and the feminine sides of their personalities, and that the neurotics of our time are the macho males and the female females, the Rambos and the Twiggies of society, which is exactly what our culture has been intent on producing.

Hospital statistics show us that prior to the women's movement 8% of the men and 20% of the women receiving psychiatric help were hospitalized for depression. But the statistics also show that following the women's movement—after women began to see opportunity and affirmation and recognition in life, just as men always have—that then, after women's liberation became a possibility, still 9% of all the men but only 8% of all the women receiving psychiatric help were hospitalized for depression.

No, science will not confirm a basis for the oppression of women. And society is certainly no sign of the inferiority of women either. Women have run governments, and discovered comets, and guided major exploratory expeditions, and counseled popes, and developed businesses, and led non-violent movements and created alternative communities in the Church—even despite the Church—and, by now, have worked in every major arena in society, at least with obvious competence, if never with equity, and, at the same time, did it all alone, and with no help from anyone.

No, society, like science, is no testimony in favor of the inherent inequality of women. And surely the best doctrines of the Church are not. We do baptize women, after all, and we insist on shriving and absolving them, and we marry them in the same full sacramental recognition that their husbands get, and we bless their bodies and reconcile their souls, and we communicate them, and we confirm them—just like the males with them—in their obligation to spread the faith as well as to keep the faith.

We say always—at least right up until where it counts—that God made women in God's own image, and that God talked to them just as God talked to men, and that God trusted them with free will just as much as God trusted men. And we say that in the Incarnation Jesus redeemed women, too, and will raise them from the dead, just as well as men, and that in their lives God gives them grace, too, though sadly it is also said that women may not be carriers of grace, or dispense it, or preach it, or use it in the Church in any official way. God's grace, it seems, goes sour when it gets to women.

But, nevertheless, the good news is that science and society and theology all say that women are grand, equal, human beings, and some women have been able to prove that's so. But the bad news is that so few women have been given the chance. So what is there left for us to do about it that will not, of course, blight the plan of God for us? Perhaps the only way to be sure that what we do in the future as women and for women will not corrupt the design of the eternal for us is to look at the women whom Yahweh raised up as models, and look at the women whom Christ affirmed and ask, first, what was the agenda of these women? And, second, has that agenda been satisfied? And, finally, if not, then what, in the name of creation, must we do about that if we are to be true both to the Gospel and to *Pacem in Terris* in which John XXIII says clearly: "Those who discover that they have rights have the responsibility to claim them?"

Let us look, for instance, at the agendas of the widows Ruth and Naomi. Naomi was a widowed old woman and Ruth was a younger one in a society that had no room for widows. Only Ruth, the younger woman, was still sexually attractive and sexually acceptable, and so she did the only thing a woman could do to take care of the people she loved more than her very own life. Ruth gave herself to a man, not for his love, not for his holy companionship, but for his money and for his security.

But our society has no room either for single women or for widows. Our young women—most of them—work in the lowest of low class jobs for the lowest of low wages, without future and without just recompense. The Bureau of Labor Statistics tells us that 80% of employed women are segregated in 20% of the 420 job categories in the United States, and that there is "women's work" even in the "non-sex-stratified" areas. In sales, for example, 83% of those who sell apparel are women who earn an average of $171 a week. But car and boat sales*men*—and 92% of them are—earn an average of $400 a week. The Bureau tells us, too, that even professional women earn only 71% of the wages earned by professional men in the same profession.

Three-fourths of our old women, the U. N. Decade on Women shows, live below the poverty line. In fact, two-thirds of the elderly women of the U.S.—the richest and supposedly the most feminist nation on earth—live on a fraction of their husbands' Social Security checks. If she dies first, of course, he will continue to receive the entire Social Security check, despite the fact that she's no longer his dependent. But if he dies first, before the age of their retirement, this society, if it gives her anything at all, for years will withhold from that woman whole portions of what should have been that check—despite inflation, despite need, despite the fact that rent and light and heat and food cost old women exactly what they cost old men. As a result, retired men in this country receive an average of $5500 a year but retired women are living on an average of only $3300 a year.

Take that information into the pulpit on Mother's Day and see if you can convince women how much church and state really value their work in the home. Oh, yes, the message about whose money their money really is, is very clear. And no, Ruth and Naomi's agenda has not been satisfied. The feminization of poverty is still with us and getting worse by the day.

But let us look, then, at the agenda of Moses' mother and Pharoah's daughter. Moses' mother and Pharoah's daughter lived in a society where "men were men," and differences were solved by destruction and might made right and the innocent were sacrificed for the sake of the powerful. Moses' mother and Pharoah's daughter wanted no part of the domination and destruction that characterize the male power paradigm. Moses' mother and Pharoah's daughter believed in compassion instead of conflict, and collaboration instead of coercion, and cooperation rather than competition. And together, secretly, those two women—one who had inherited a destructive system and one who was being oppressed by that destructive system—reached across the boundaries of their separated world to redeem it by refusing to be enemies, by saving the child and therefore saving the race.

Well, our society doesn't want the woman's viewpoint in conflict resolution situations and important social arenas either. Women aren't tough enough, they fear, to push the nuclear button—in some circles, apparently, a skill to be envied. Our society, in fact, works hard to glorify the masculine ideal, and institutionalize male modes of response and denigrate feminine values and smile-down feminine strategies and dismiss feminine social models. Our society works hard, as a result, to take the "woman" out of the recruit, to make a boy a man, and to make the man a killer. Our society plans, in fact, to eliminate 100% of the women and children of the world in the nuclear wars men have designed to "protect" them. And no one is even asking those women if that is all right!

There is no doubt about it, the agenda of Moses' mother and Pharoah's daughter has definitely not been satisfied. The theology of domination and the machomania it breeds is with us still and threatens now not simply a people but an entire globe.

But let us look, then, at the agenda of Esther, the woman who is expected to be an ornament in the court of the king. They call her "queen" but only in things that do not matter to an autocratic and hierarchial world. "No one can go to the king," she reports to the people who look to her for help, "unless the king calls them. And I have not been called to the palace of the king for over 30 days." And then risks her life to do what must be done.

In our society, too, women may give advice—when and if they're ever asked—but women are seldom official advisors, except in token ways, and women are almost never decision makers. Only 10% of the government positions in this country are held by women; and only 5% of the corporate executive positions are held by women; and no percentage at all of the decision-making positions of the Church are held by women.

Like Esther, what women finally do for right and truth they do at their own peril. They can lose their homes and their jobs and their reputations and their faith for it because no one is really obliged to listen. They can wear their bodies and their hearts and their souls completely out trying to be heard but no one, absolutely no one, is obliged either to hear or to respond.

By all means, be clear about this: Whatever now the number of token women in the boardrooms and the chanceries of the world, Esther's agenda of influence and presence and participation in the charism of power has definitely not been satisfied. It is the males of the system who shape, control, administer and own it. Sometimes beneficently, true, but always totally and finally.

But let us look, then, at the agenda of Judith. Judith wanted the harassment and brutality to stop once and for all. Judith wanted to be free of male intimidation and male bondage and male abuse and male threat. And in desperation, but with deep faith, she finally confronts it. She goes to the enemy camp without male protection and puts an end to the abuse and wins the salvation of the city.

But in this country yet, according to Geller, Steinmetz and Brown in *Behind Closed Doors*, two million women are beaten yearly because men "take dominion" over women's bodies, and men have forever encouraged men to do so in booty, in brothels and in economic bondage.

In 2/3 of all marriages, women are beaten at least once; 1/4 of the women of this country are beaten weekly; 20% of all the emergency medical services given to women follow a beating; 25% of all the female suicide attempts are a result of repeated domestic beatings; 25% of all female murder victims are murdered either by their husbands or their boyfriends. A woman in this country is beaten every 18 seconds and raped every three minutes. Pornographers make $4 billion dollars every single year on the abuse of women. Violence toward women in this country and in every country is not sometimes. Violence against women is always.

No, indeed, Judith's agenda of freedom and personal security has definitely not been satisfied for women.

So let us look, then, at the agendas of Mary of Bethany and the Samaritan woman and Mary Magdalen and the women at the tomb. The Samaritan woman simply didn't fit any of their social standards. Mary of Bethany simply didn't accept any of their role definitions. Mary Magdalen was indeed a bold and brazen woman. And they made no bones—any of them—about their commitment to Jesus. No bones at all about either his call or their intention—in fact, their compulsion—to carry on his will and his wonderful presence in their lives.

The Samaritan woman faced them head on. Mary of Bethany persisted in her vocation. The women of Jerusalem went on ministering to him while all the others hid. Mary Magdalen, remember, went right into their midst—it was a forty-hours gathering, or perhaps a synod, I think—to minister to him and to proclaim his Resurrection.

"What is that woman doing in here," the men said. "Send her away." And they went to the tomb to see for themselves, "because they did not believe her," the Scripture reads. "We have no more need of you," the men of Samaria said. "Our place is in the kitchen," Martha, the well-conditioned woman, said.

But Jesus said back to all of them: "She is doing what you are not doing; she's preparing me for my burial." And Jesus said, "But she has chosen the better part, and it shall not be denied her."

And Jesus said to the woman, and to the woman only, "I am the Messiah." And Jesus said, "Mary, don't stay here. You go and tell Peter and the others . . . ."

Well, we live in a society where women are still not allowed into the Holy of Holies. We live in a society where they turn women away from their empty seminaries in droves, while in a sacramental Church people lack the sacraments.

We live in a society where a girl-child, ironically, may not even officially carry a cruet to the altar, because the Church that teaches "that the gates of hell shall not prevail against it" can, apparently, be brought to its knees by a little 11-year-old girl.

We live in a society where women are no longer allowed to preach the Gospel, or minister the sacraments to the dying, or teach Scripture to the ordinandi. And if and when they do, they do not believe her. Oh, yes, the message is very clear and it is still the same: There is nothing that a man of the Church can learn about God and faith and Gospel from a woman of the Church. Never forget, full inclusion in ministry was the agenda of Mary Magdalen and Mary of Bethany and the Samaritan woman and the women at the tomb, and that agenda, 2000 years later, is not yet satisfied, despite the words of Jesus.

Let us look, too, at the agenda of Eve, the mother of the human race. Eve was created, like Adam, directly by God. Eve was given paradise, like Adam, and on a par with him. And Adam, like Eve, heard the serpent. And Adam, like Eve, sinned anyway. And Eve, like Adam, was gloriously redeemed.

But when history tells the story of Eve, there is little recognition that the sin was, after all, only half hers. Neither Adam nor Eve, after all, kept the commandment of God—they both heard the temptation together and neither one of them refused—nor did he even question, the big rational hunk: "Now, Honey, you know how emotional you get about these things; let's talk about it tonight after supper . . ." Even, surely, the office for the Doctrine of the Faith is willing to admit that they found two sets of teeth marks on the apple.

Indeed, the result of that joint sin was the rupture of relationships between human beings and God, and between the human beings themselves. But if that is so, then redemption depends on our transcending and repairing the ruptures, not on our institutionalizing them. But we still live in a world where the official texts of the Church say only that women, as a result of the sin, are devoted to less noble ends than men. And on the basis of that reasoning, women are still being denied education and autonomy and economic independence and full human adulthood this whole world over.

And no one has officially declared those texts wrong.

You bet the agenda of Eve—the recognition of women's real moral equality—is long unfinished.

Finally, let us look, as well, at the agenda of Mary, the Mother of God; Mary, the unmarried mother; Mary, the political refugee; Mary, the homeless one; Mary, the disciple and prophet; Mary, the Third World woman; Mary, the one full of grace.

Mary simply took things into her own hands. The standards of the society and the norms of the synagogue meant absolutely nothing to her next to the deep, clear, commanding call of God in her life. Mary knew that what the law demanded she could not do, because what God asked she must do under any circumstances. Mary knew that the gift given to her by God had to be brought to fruit, no matter who thought otherwise.

Mary's agenda was fullness of personhood. Mary was the liberated and the liberator. Mary changed God into the body and blood of Christ; she called for miracles and got them; she made the *Magnificat* the national anthem of women everywhere.

And yet, still, this very day, women are being married for dowry and sold for bride-price and denied an inheritance and deprived of money and work and land and housing and food stamps and child care services and health and welfare benefits. And they are sacrificed daily in one way and another for the political, military, economic and theological sins of men. And what are we doing about it?

Oh, indeed, the agenda of the 90s is far too clear because it is far too long in being satisfied. The women raised up before us by God—Ruth and Naomi and Moses' mother and Pharoah's daughter and Esther and the Samaritan woman and Mary of Bethany and Mary Magdalen and Eve, the mother of the human race, and Mary, the Mother of God—have spoken to every century about the needs and rights and burdens of being woman. Over and over they call to us about the feminization of poverty, the destructiveness of the theology of domination, the destructive lack of participation in the power that rules them, the need for affirmation of the feminine, full inclusion in ministry, the recognition of basic moral equality and fullness of female personhood. And what the Church teaches and models about women's nature, place and role gives credibility or contradiction to these realities; in this generation, too, though we may have awareness, we definitely do not have equality.

The question of the 90s is creation. The agenda for the 90s is to claim it fully. Everywhere.

But to do that as Church we must have a new theology of family and a new kind of Cana conferences where the concepts of mutuality and parenting bring truth to old, unfit, one- sided notions of obedience and mothering. We must write and research and question the limited states of women's lives until the questions are heard and the answers make both good sense and good church.

We must give the lie to the lies. We must press for a resolution of the tension between the definition of Church and the practice of clericalism. We must be about the retelling of Scripture in ways that give light to the dignity and the dreams and the gifts of women there and everywhere. We must link and bond together to affirm and promote the hopes and the needs and the rights of women who, regardless of how comfortable you and I may see our own individual lives, are as a class still degraded, rejected, ignored, used, exploited, deluded, homeless and poor.

Most of all, we must not let ourselves be divided from one another in our struggle for women everywhere. We must, if no one else will, hear the voices of women that sound different from our own and care about hurts unlike our own until all women's concerns are seen as human concerns.

We must reassess the meaning of the Incarnation and its implications for ministry. We must as Church bring ourselves to choose between sacraments and maleness. We must see the links between militarization and the domination and deprivation of women and their children around the entire globe. We must realize that women of color are doubly burdened, and do everything possible to end our own national policies of economic deprivation and social irresponsibility which contribute to that.

And, finally, we must, if we cannot change them, change ourselves, which is to say that we must, after all this time, wait no longer to refuse abuse and refuse victimization and refuse trivialization and refuse the invisibility that invades every institution in society, even the language of the Church. And we must find nonviolent ways to do so.

We must begin to target our donations for women's projects; we must make public our discontent and disapproval of the absence of women from important state and Church affairs; we must swamp the chanceries and congresses and corporations of the world with petitions for change.

And finally, in the face of opposition, we must not give up. We must develop the virtue of tenacity. We must develop strong organizations of women. We must support the ones that already exist, weary after years of effort in our behalf. We must educate the next generation to understand why what is, is. And we must take as our lifelong truth: "If not for us, then because of us." We must question and claim and care enough to go on when going on seems fruitless. And most of all, we must not be silent. We must speak up and speak to and speak on until sexism is seen for the sin it is and repented.

That is the agenda for them as Church and for us as Church, all together and alone.

It is not that much has not already been said on women. It is simply that it is not possible to have a conscience and say nothing. When Jesus was crucified, many "followed at a distance," Scripture records, but they are not the ones we remember, nor are they the ones we emulate, nor are they the ones who stand for the best in the Church. It was two women and one non-violent male who went all the way to the foot of the cross, professing truth publicly.

Well, once again, we need women of courage and men of conscience to bring the tenor of truth to a time when turning back is impossible and turning to is unclear.

And is there any hope at all? Well, only this perhaps, but good enough for me. Remember, on the hard days, that when the church of Jerusalem debated the legitimacy of accepting Gentiles into Jewish Christianity, the struggle was bitter. Jesus had never done it, they argued. Judaism was for the Jews, they argued. But Peter proclaimed then: "If God was giving them the same gift we were given, who was I to interfere." And Gamaliel argued, when the Jews resisted new revelation, "Let these people alone. If their purpose or activity is human in its origins, it will destroy itself. If, on the other hand, it comes from God, you will not be able to destroy them without fighting God." (Acts, 5:38) In both instances, the men of the church were converted from smothering the spirit of God. My hope is that the men of the church can be converted again.

But most of all, my hope lies in the sign of a woman whose life was also finally unbent.

The Scripture reads: "On a Sabbath Day Jesus was teaching in one of the synagogues. There was a woman there who for 18 years had been possessed by a spirit which drained her strength. She was badly stooped, quite incapable of standing erect. And when Jesus saw her, he called her to him and said, 'Woman, you are free of your infirmity.' And he laid his hand upon her and immediately she stood up straight and began thanking God." (John 13:10)

Indeed, there is great hope. All we need in this next decade are the prophetic insights of Peter and Gamaliel, the faith of the afflicted woman, the memory of Jesus and the courage of the powerless who went protesting publicly to the foot of the cross.

"To be born a woman," the holy one said, "is not destiny. To be born a woman is fate. Destiny is what you make of it."

"There is no cure," the Africans say, "that does not cost." The cure the Church needs now may well cost many of us, but that will be little enough price to pay for a goal so great, the Church—full, equal and undivided.

This time it is you whom the next generation will thank or not for both the conscience and the courage it will take to unbend their stooped lives.

3
Woman: Icon, Rebel, Saint

The role and place of women in church and society is a good news/bad news presentation.

The good news is that great women have always walked the earth; that their footprints are still clear; that their presence has changed things both in church and in society. The good news, never to be forgotten, is Mary, Phoebe, Prisca, Junia and Thecla, the founders, teachers and deaconesses of the early church. The good news is Marthana, the fifth-century church administrator who was a quasi-episcopal abbess, and superior of a dual monastery of both men and women. The good news is the Byzantine empress, Theodora, who freed the prostitutes of Constantinople from the dungeons ascribed to them by the men who used them. The good news is the church leader, Hilda, an abbess of the seventh century and a delegate to the church's Synod of Whitby.

The good news is the tenth-century feminist-dramatist-nun, Hrotswitha, who wrote plays in the classical style of Terrence and challenged sexism directly by claiming both her talent and her responsibility to it: "Those who obstruct my God-given gifts," she wrote, "do so at the risk of God's judgement." The good news is the Dutch Scripture scholar, Anna van Schurman, who argued for the education of women with all the major figures of 17th-century Europe. The good news is the 18th-century American Indian woman, Sacajawea, the chief interpreter, guide and protector of the Lewis and Clark expedition which opened the entire Northwest Territory but who, despite it all, was never paid and never recognized for those brave and skillful services. The good news is the astronomer, Caroline Herschel, the 19th-century woman who discovered eight comets, but who received only "honorary" recognition from the Royal Astrological Society of Hanover, Germany, because that most prestigious society was open "to men only." The good news is the abolitionist and feminist, Sojourner Truth, who demanded human liberty and spoke out for the freedom of slaves and the full humanity of black and white women everywhere. The good news is Dr. Elizabeth Blackwell, the first woman in the United States to be a licensed, practicing physician, though they destroyed her office and drove her out of New York City bodily in the early 20th century because the fine upstanding men of the commonwealth, defenders of human standards all, said it was immoral for a woman to be a doctor.

The good news is Catherine of Siena, who counseled a pope, whether he wanted her counsel or not; Teresa of Avila, who reformed the religious life of the church, whether they said it should be reformed or not; Joan of Arc, who claimed direct authority and power from God, whether they said that women could have power and authority or not; Mary Ward, who contested with cardinals of the Church, whether they ceded the contest or not; and Dorothy Day, who called both country and Church to account for their misuse of power, whether they would admit it or not. The good news is a host of women over time who have resisted and confronted both church and state to be what God called them to be. The good news is our own grandmothers and great-grandmothers who struggled for the suffrage that you and I now take for granted. The good news is that despite pressure, despite rejection, despite false theologies of creation and false biologies of women, women keep pressing, keep turning, keep thirsting toward fullness of life and the pulse of holy power.

At the same time, the bad news is that in so many years so few women have ever come to know the opportunities, the recognition and the holy power they deserved. The bad news for all of us, both men and women, at this moment in history is that the feminine in life has been suppressed over and over again and this time, perhaps, to our peril.

The new news is that the future of society itself may depend on the position this generation takes on the question of the role of women. The new news is that our generation, as never before, is being forced to choose, woman as icon, woman as rebel or woman as saint. Two ancient stories illustrate best, perhaps, the depth of the struggle.

In the first story, the disciple asked the elder, "Holy one, what must I do to be enlightened?" And the elder said, "To be enlightened, you must make a clean break with your weaker past." And the disciple answered, "Well, I am doing that, little by little." But the elder replied: "No one crossed a chasm little by little. To get across a chasm you must take a leap." In the second parable, the disciples ask the elder to talk to them about power, and the sage said, "Once upon a time, there was a snake in the village that had bitten so many people that few dared to go into the fields. So the village holy one tamed the snake and persuaded it to practice the discipline of non-violence. Well, it did not take long for the people to see that the snake had become harmless, and soon all the men and even the children of the town took to hurling stones at the snake and dragging it by its tail. One day, the holy one found the snake, badly bruised and bleeding, lying in a ditch on the side of the road. 'Friend, whatever has happened to you?' the holy one asked. And the snake said, 'I've been passive and gentle and uncomplaining like you told me to be.' 'Oh dear,' the holy one said, 'there's been a terrible mistake. I only told you to stop hurting. I never said to stop hissing.'"

The points are clear. First, for life to be life, we must take the leap and live it to the fullest. Secondly, for a person to be a person and not a victim or a scapegoat, we must claim our power and use it well. But the problems are clear, too. We have to know what the leap requires. We have to know what kind of power we're talking about. We have to know what it means to be icon, rebel and saint before we choose to be any of them. But where shall we go to discover the differences among them? And what do they have to say to us in our time as church and society? My suggestion is that we look to Scripture to find both a model and a meaning of new life and new power for women.

I suggest as model of woman as icon, Susanna, the wife of Joachim and the daughter of Hilkiah. I suggest as model of woman as rebel, Judith, the widow of Bethulia. And, finally, I suggest as model of woman as saint, Mary, the mother of Jesus.

In Daniel 13, Susanna is a chauvinist's dream of an icon. She is a madonna figure of grand design—attacked but innocent, threatened but faithful. She is assaulted by two friends of her husband's in his own home. And, faced with public punishment or personal ravishment, Susanna chooses death rather than dishonor. Indeed, Susanna is a perfect picture of the woman that men have made up for women to be. The Scripture details quite clearly her innocence (she is not flirting), her vulnerability (she is alone), and, worse, perhaps, her total dependence on men both for her value and her vindication. "Submit to us," the molesting old men say, "or we will defame you and bring you to death." Like any good icon, Susanna was an image of the ideal, the other-worldly, the frilly feminine of life. She stayed at home and walked in her garden. She was demure and devoted, docile and proper, pure and powerless. "I am completely trapped," Susanna says. "If I yield, it will be my death. If I refuse, I cannot escape your power." And so Susanna was prey, despite her dutifulness and perhaps because of it, to the powerful lusts of men. And, indeed, the icon Susanna is with us still.

Susanna lives in every woman whose dependence renders her powerless to be what she should be and to do what she should do. Susanna lives in India and is killed for bride-price or starved to feed her husband. Susanna lives in Japan and is prostituted for the sake of "the recreational opportunities" afforded Western business firms, for the sake of profit. Susanna lives in the Americas where she is commonly abandoned and usually left without alimony; where she is beaten by husbands and boyfriends every 18 seconds, the statistics say, while the courts wrestle with whether or not "domestic assault" is really a criminal offense.

Oh, yes, Susanna is the model woman who gets saved by men and scolded by men and slighted by men and slapped by men, who have all learned well that they have not only a right but a responsibility to own and sell and command and control and direct and determine and destroy whatever is theirs. And the Susannas of the world are definitely theirs because it is centuries of male biology and male theology and male philosophy and male legislation that have deftly created them.

When Plato categorized women with children and animals in the *Thaetetus*, and taught in the *Timaeus* that women are created from wicked men as a man's punishment for being irrational, and when he declared in *The Republic* that "There is nothing that women as a class can do better than men as a class, even in spheres reserved for women," Susanna was forever cast as derivative and deficient, without real human role or genuine skills and personal gifts. And history says that Plato's position on women was ahead of its time.

When Aristotle taught that "All of nature and most humans are simply instruments meant to supply necessities and comforts for the higher class," and when he observed that "the world is naturally divided into natural rulers and the naturally ruled, and that hierarchical order is good for both the slaves and for the women," then, at that moment, all the judges and the guardians and the molesters and the spokes*men* and the chair*men* and the mail*men*, the entire patriarchal family, were both created and legitimated.

When Thomas Aquinas taught that in the process of reproduction, females were responsible for the human body but that male semen was the raw material of the human soul and that women did not have "sufficient strength of mind to resist concupiscence," all the violence of the world was released against Susanna. Even civil law recognized "the rule of thumb" which gave a man the right to beat his wife "for Godly chastisement" as long as the weapon he used was no bigger around than his thumb. And the legal system concurred.

Indeed, all the Susannas of the world are trapped. Except for the rebels. For if Daniel:13, the story of Susanna, is the stuff of icons, then the Book of Judith is a handbook for rebels, for women who are achievers, doers, non-conformists and bearers of the restless urge to humanhood. It is a handbook for those who are bearers of the compelling call to live out the Word of God in their lives immediately, not vicariously, by means of their own calls, not simply through the lives of others. In Judith, God delivers the Jewish people through the instrumentality of a woman. Here, as surely as God worked through Moses, God works through Judith as well.

Cut off from water by siege for 34 days, the people of Bethulia are desperate and on the verge of surrender. All the tactics of the past have failed; the plans of men have turned to nothing; all their power ploys have come to grief. Until the woman, Judith, comes to do "a man's work" a woman's way. She takes to the camp of the enemy a maid-servant instead of an army. She makes herself a friend instead of an enemy. She pits her brain against his brawn and she overcomes him, liberates the people and saves the city. Judith, who should have been at home, who had no proper part of the public world, the law said, whose place was off the streets and in the outer court of the temple, this woman who was, the Scripture says, "a very God-fearing woman" was, perhaps, a bold one. She was also a persistent one. "Listen to me," she said to the leaders of the city. "I will do something that will go down from generation to generation among the descendants of our race."

And that night Judith did what the men of the place could not do. She called upon God to fulfill the gift that had been given her: "Give me, a widow, the strong hand to execute my plan . . . . Your strength is not in numbers, nor does your power depend upon stalwart men; but you are the God of the lowly, the helper of the oppressed, the supporter of the weak, the protector of the forsaken, the savior of those without hope." And Holofernes fell, however sad the way, to the rebel woman, Judith.

And she has been followed in every generation of rebel women after her who knew themselves also to be exiles in a male world. They rebelled against the physiology that taught that brainwork rendered a woman sterile; they rebelled against the theology that taught that woman's only role was motherhood; they rebelled against the idolatry that made God's graven image male. They rebelled against pornography and domestic rape and slave wages and war. They went to jail for the vote and to Congress for equality and to school for education and to work for economic independence.

And, historians are discovering, along the way they fashioned achievements to live forever. In Vare and Ptacek's *Mothers of Invention: A History of Forgotten Women and Their Unforgettable Ideas*, we find that the culture-changing machine credited to Eli Whitney as

the cotton gin was really conceived, perfected and marketed by
Catherine Littlefield. We know now that it was a woman who
patented the Navy's first signal flare; it was a woman who intro-
duced smallpox inoculation; it was a woman who perfected solar
heating and created the basis of computer software and developed
refrigeration and produced the first usable penicillin and designed
the first tract housing and discovered radioactivity and created, and
named, nuclear fission.

But the painting depicting America's great inventors in the
Smithsonian Institution, called "Men of Progress," is that indeed for
it shows men and men only. To this day. Now. 1988. And then they
have the nerve to say "What else do women want?" And they call
them rebels and viragos, and Amazons, and radical feminists and
unnatural women. How many of them are there now? Well, in a
Gallup poll of five years ago, only 20% of women sampled called
themselves "feminist," but over 80% of them accepted every item on
the National Women's Agenda. A similar survey conducted several
years later indicated that, of women over 50, only 22% of the
women described themselves as feminist, but 57% of the women in
their 20s said they were. And that is the stuff of which rebellion is
made. And these rebellious women, the U. N. Decade on Women
discovered, are in Asia and Africa and India and Italy and England
and South America. And here, right here, now.

Why? Because as long as Schopenhauer's notion that a woman is
by nature deficient carries more weight in the structures of this
society than Mary Wollenstonecraft's contention that opportunity
determines capacity; as long as Nietzche's position that "Women
should be brought up as dangerous playthings for the relaxation of
the soldier" is more institutionalized than John Stuart Mill's analysis
that no society can be called just as long as half its people, women,
are kept in subjection; as long as Freud's position that women simply want to be men is more credible than Karen Horney's or Alfred
Adler's thesis that women suffer from the same kind of suppressed
ambitions common to any class of oppressed people, then, absolutely, the rebel Judith will live, struggling to be all that she is capable of
being. And often, out of her frustration, in ways considered radical
or unnatural or uncouth or even immoral. But why the fear or resis-

tance? If women are really as bad as men have said they are, then surely it won't be necessary to suppress them. They'll fail anyway.

Until then, what shall we do? My hope is that we will raise up saints, women who are holy blends of the icon and the rebel; women who give us both models of the feminine face of God and the power of the Spirit; women who make the improbable possible; women who defy the system for the sake of the sacred in life; women who, like Mary of Nazareth, break through all the gossamer layers of false femaleness to bring feminine strength to a world in danger of destruction from the institutionalization of masculine values; women who will bring peace to a planet reeling from macho-mania, with the confidence of the *Magnificat* singing in their souls.

Mary of Nazareth knew very well what it meant to be strong: She was strong enough to know that she had been favored by God when the society said she couldn't be so favored and the tradition said she wouldn't be so favored. She was strong enough to realize the strength of another woman when she went to Elizabeth for support and affirmation rather than to the synagogue to try to persuade the priests of the legitimacy of their visions, or to the government for protection, or even to the men to whom they were espoused to explain or cajole or plead. No, these two women, Mary and Elizabeth, simply do what they must do together and leave it to the rest of us to do the same. Mary was strong enough to strike out in uncertainty, secure in her call. She was strong enough to bring the right concerns, the right questions, the right witness, the right insight into our world, even if it meant questioning the angels. At Cana she was strong enough to insist on miracles and to get them. There were two miracles. We talk about only one. First: changing of water into wine; second, a woman becomes a leader in the Christian church. There in the midst of those who called themselves the disciples, she was strong enough to withstand the natural order of things so that the new order could be a better order. She was strong enough to bridge two worlds without losing the better part of either one. She was strong enough never to give up, not to be afraid, to begin over again and again and again, after Bethlehem, and after Egypt and after the crucifixion. She knew who she was and she let neither the society nor the synagogue tell her otherwise, though she stood for the best in both. She brought the power of the icon and the power of the rebel to white heat. Mary of Nazareth made feminism an article of the faith, and power holy. Mary shows us the sanctifying power of a human being who has become fully human.

The psychiatrist, Rollo May, tells us quite clearly that there are five kinds of power. I'm suggesting the type of power we choose determines whether we will be icon, rebel or saint. The first type of power, exploitative power, is the kind of power that uses force against others for personal gain. Slavery, white minority rule of native majorities for production and profit without full citizenship and economic participation are kinds of exploitative power. The second type of power, manipulative power, controls others for personal gain through tokenism or propaganda. Tokenism allows a few people into the center of the system without being accused of doing it. Tokenism is one woman on the President's cabinet, or one woman in a spacecraft, or one woman on the parish council, or one woman on the staff. The figures show, in fact, that a woman with a college degree will earn on the average $2,000 less per year than a man who dropped out of high school at the age of 16. Indeed, tokenism is destructive.

Propaganda, the other kind of manipulative power, manipulates by dinning into the minds of people the fear of "The Communist Threat," for instance, when it is our own first-strike weapons that will destroy us; propaganda plies us with the threat of "Radical Feminism" when feminism is simply a commitment to the equality, dignity and full humanity of all persons to such a degree that we work to bring about the structural changes that will make that possible. Manipulative propaganda makes sure that we never imagine the warmth of the Soviet people or recognize the commonplace of intelligent women or the liberation of the human spirit that comes for both women and men in feminism.

The third type of power, competitive power, works against others to defeat them. Competitive power is the need to be number one, on top, head of the house, the boss. The arms race with its stockpiles far beyond defense, let alone security, is pure competitive power. We live in a world where the end of the world has been created and is being stored in the cornfields of Kansas. And every day we go on creating destruction over and over again. Government interference in Vietnam and Chile and Nicaragua is competitive power. Barring women from clubs and unions and job categories is competitive power. Two-thirds of the poor of the world are women because they can't get the same kinds of work or salaries or promotions that men can. In the United States alone, that bastion of women's rights, they say, over half of the women of the country are in the work force, but less than 20% are in management positions and that a mere 10% more women managers than we had in 1971. And in the categories that do employ women, women are still the lowest paid.

Clearly, exploitation and competition and manipulation are destroying us at every level just as they destroyed both Susanna and Judith. But there are two kinds of power, nurturing power and integrative power, that bring woman as icon and woman as rebel into the sanctity needed for our time. Mary used her power to empower others, to bring things together and, as a result, to enable fullness of life for everyone. Parenting and education and advocacy and solidarity with the poor are types of nurturing power. Mary's power to say yes in a world that demanded that she say no made her something new, and in the process, made the whole world new with her. Like the seeker of enlightenment, Mary took the leap for us away from the bloodless icon, away from isolated rebel to saint, to a holy one of God, by being everything she was meant to be. And she showed us that we can be it, too. The fact is that Mary is not simply "Mary, the Mother of God." No, on the contrary. The Mother of God is the image of women everywhere. The Mother of God is Mary, independent woman; Mary, the unmarried mother; Mary, the homeless woman; Mary, the political refugee; Mary, the Third World woman; Mary, the mother of the condemned; Mary, the widow who outlives her child; Mary, the woman of our time who shares in the divine plan of salvation; Mary, the bearer of Christ.

She stands as icon among the women of the world and calls to rebellion the women of the world who live in subjection or suppression. She calls the typical rural African woman who works 17 hours a day, and the Asian women who account for at least 50% of the food production of their countries but get none of the income from it, and the 1/3 of the women world-wide who are the sole supporters of their families, not women working for luxuries, not women working for pin money, but women working for food!—but who work without day care centers or equal pay or health and pension benefits. She is the saintly icon who breaks out of lifeless molds and makes rebellion plain to the legions of women whose supportive husbands pride themselves on their feminism because, actually, they "allow" their wives to work two jobs: one job to help pay the bills and the other to maintain the home by cooking and cleaning and washing and taking care of the children after the first job is done. And alone.

The peace movement and civil rights and feminism are all types of integrating power that make life whole and make life holy. It is our call, too, to practice the power that makes all things new so that others, all others, women as well as men, may have life and have it more abundantly. That's the good news.

The bad news, for all of us, men and women alike, at this moment in history is that the feminine in life has been made into an icon, or repressed into rebellion, and suppressed in all our systems over and over again, so that, as a result, humanity walks on one leg, sees with one eye, and thinks with one half of the human mind, and, consequently perhaps, stands on the brink of its own extermination.

Clearly, today's militarism is not based on national defense. We obviously have more than enough weapons for defense and, in fact, for the destruction of the entire globe. No, today's militarism is based on national determinations to control resources and markets and profits and power for a few. Today's militarism is based on male values run amok. Today's militarism is based on domination of inferiors by those who tell themselves that God made them superior and in charge.

Consequently, women are poor and minority women are poorest of all. People are out of work and women are the most underpaid of all. Money is being taken away from human service and poured into the fine art of planetary destruction, and women and minority peoples are the most deprived of all.

And through it still, tokenism reigns supreme, even in the Church: an icon here, a rebel there; middle management maybe, nothing serious; women lectors but not altar girls, catechists but not deaconesses, women principals but not women priests, though, the seminaries are empty and women's hearts are full of call.

Why? Because the theology of domination reigns supreme. Today's world, in other words, is based on exploitative and competitive and manipulative power when it is nurturance of a devastated globe and integration of divided peoples and personal gifts that are necessary. As in Judith's time, competition, conformity and coercion have not worked. What the world needs now are the feminine values of compassion, and concensus and cooperation if the world is to survive and creation is to be fully created.

Integrity and nurturing power are the mark of the holy. Jesus called the entire Christian community, women as well as men; Mary of Bethany as well as Peter; the woman with the issue of blood as well as the man with leprosy; the daughter of Jairus as well as the son of the centurion; Mary as well as Joseph to know their power, like his, to change the face of history.

It is our duty as well. We must give up being icons and refuse to ignore our rebels and insist in ourselves on the sanctity it will take to integrate all, to nurture humanity, to repeal laws and provide equal opportunities, to change images in language and envision new roles and challenge systems, to refuse victimization and demand economic equality, and to renew our theology and refashion our relationships so that we can be friends together, neither of us either too reviled, or too revered. Saints speak out, speak up and speak on until the world transcends the sin of sexism and all God's creation is nurtured and integrated. And that demands women of courage to critique their lives and men of conscience to call their own systems.

The essayist Rosten wrote once: "The purpose of life is not to be happy; the purpose of life is to matter, to have it make a difference that you lived at all." It is time for our generation to make a difference. It is time to take the leap; it is time to change things. It is time to turn our icons and our rebels into saints. It is that for which, with Susanna, we struggle and it is that for which, with Judith, we hope. It is that for which, with Mary, we contend. And contend. And contend.

4

What's Right with the Catholic Church?

There are two stories that form the framework of these remarks. The first is from personal experience:

It was the spring of 1984. I was sitting on a stage at Stanford University. The hall seemed like a black cave to me. All I could see were high-wattage Klieg lights and, far in the back, the outline of exit signs over the auditorium doors. I had just delivered a kind of summary closing address to the public session of a three-day symposium on "Communities of Women." The symposium had been organized by the research arm of *Signs*, a journal then located at Stanford University and entirely devoted to interdisciplinary scholarship on questions of women in culture and society. Women from all over the bay area were in attendance and the vibrations of feminism were running a very heady high.

It was as if the outside world with all of its institutionalized sexism no longer existed; that this was the real world where competent women recognized and respected competent women; that the millenium had finally come.

And there sat I in the midst of it, sisterhood brimming over until suddenly a voice out of the darkness on the other side of the lights called me very quickly and very firmly back to the real world.

"Sister Joan," the voice said, "I would like to ask you a personal question. How and why does a woman like you stay in the Catholic Church?"

The message was very, very clear. I had heard many times before all the tones of passion and anger and pain that underlay the question. And then the woman's voice went on:

41

"I was a Catholic once," she said, "and the misogyny was so bad I knew it was either get out or have a breakdown. I would like to know how and why," she repeated, "someone like you stays in a church like that?"

The second story from Sufi religious literature is, I believe, an answer to the first. This story tells that a seeker arrived at the monastery in search of a spiritual guide.

"People say that you have found wisdom," the seeker said to the Holy One, "and I have come to ask if that is true?"

"You could say so," the Holy One said in a matter-of-fact kind of way.

"But what makes one wise?" the disciple asked.

"Wisdom," the Holy One said, "is simply the ability to recognize."

"I know that," the disciple said, "but the question is to recognize what?"

"Spiritual wisdom," the Holy One said, "is the ability to recognize the butterfly in a caterpillar, the eagle in an egg, the saint in the sinner."

I know intuitively—at least where women and the Church are concerned—that the Holy One is right. I find myself, as a Christian feminist, in the peculiar position of someone who sees the unseen. Like a boater out of sight of land, I have been taken—and by the very same current—away from one shore to the edges of a distant other, in storm and in darkness, but with confidence and a good compass.

The fact is that I am a feminist precisely because I am a Catholic—not as a reaction to what is wrong about the Church, but actually as a response to what is right about the Church. My Christian feminist commitment to the equality, the dignity and the humanity of all persons and the need to change structures to make that so does not come as a result of my rejection of what I see as bad in the Church. It comes as an inevitable recognition of what I see as the great, the magnetizing, the empowering, the energizing good that is inherent for women in the Church and promised for women in the Church, even when I cannot see it yet being brought to fullness, even in the Church.

The fact is that what is right about the Church for women is the vision of Jesus. And everything it manifests. And everything it mandates.

Jesus, we must always remember, was a good Jew. Jesus went up to the temple, and taught the Torah, and kept the high holydays, and went on pilgrimage to Jerusalem, and studied the law. Jesus knew what was expected of him and Jesus did it. Except, of course, when an even greater revelation of the will of God demanded change. It is in those very departures by Jesus from Jewish revelation to new insights about the mind of God that we see most clearly the Christian dispensation.

So, to understand the impact of what Jesus does we must understand what Jesus is expected to do. We must remember well that Jesus' Jewish culture and Jewish religion were very clear about women. The culture and religious code in which Jesus was formed—and which we can expect him to honor unless, of course, it is those very concepts that must be challenged with a fuller notion of the will of God—left little doubt about the role and place of women.

"Better that the Torah be burned than placed in the mouth of a woman," the rabbis preached. Woman's place is in the home or in the outer court of the temple, the Law said. Women's bodies were polluted and polluting, the Torah taught. Women were not to speak to men in public—not to their husbands, not to their fathers, not to their sons.

Women were for childbearing, not for thinking, the scholars said. Women were domestic servants, not developed adults. Women were for inheritance and for convenience—not for religion, not for law. "When a boy child comes, peace comes," the rabbis taught; "when a girl child comes, nothing comes."

Oh, yes, Jesus knew church law about women, all right. And then despite it all, in great, grandiose, graphic gestures, Jesus came and swept it all away. Jesus spoke to women in public, Jesus let women follow him out of the house, Jesus discussed theology with women, and sought out their companionship, and valued their friendship, and Jesus told women—and only women—that he was the Messiah. And Jesus sent women to give testimony to his Resurrection; Jesus sent women as apostles to the apostles.

It was women who anointed him, and women who proclaimed him, and women who prepared him for burial, and women who pronounced his return.

It was women, in fact, whom Jesus put at the very center of the only two mysteries of the faith that are basic and essentially differentiating to the faith—the Incarnation and the Resurrection. And not only were women there at the Incarnation and the Resurrection, but only women were there.

Jesus taught women: "Mary has chosen the better part and it shall not be denied her," he said of the woman learning at his feet.

"Go and tell the others what you have heard," he missioned the Samaritan woman as first evangelist to the non-Jew.

"Arise and walk," he said to the corpse of a dead and worthless woman.

"Do whatever she tells you," he instructed the men servants.

"And there were women in the crowd," Scripture reads. "And women followed him, ministering to him," Scripture reads. "Woman, your faith has made you whole," Scripture reads. "And power went out of him to her," the Scripture reads.

Oh, yes, if you are a woman, the images are strong, and bold, and clear, and empowering, and life-giving and preserved by the Church. Etched on our minds forever, thanks to the Scriptures of the Church, are the figures of the strong, present, prophetic women of the Gospels.

Never forget:

• A woman with the same power to say NO to God as the power given to Abraham and Moses;

• A woman turning God into the body and blood of Christ;

• A woman, Anna, proclaiming the birth of the Messiah;

• The woman evangelist sent from the well to convert an entire city in Samaria;

• Women demanding miracles and getting them;

• Women anointing him and preparing him for burial;

• Women waiting faithfully at the empty tomb;

• Women clinging to the Risen Christ;

• Women sent "to tell Peter and the others."

Indeed, when the Church and its documents and its structures and its symbols and its language and its laws and its liturgies forgets or foregoes or forswears the place of women in the Christian dispensation, there in its Scriptures the vision of Jesus with women stays vibrant and vital and unable to be forgotten. And without it, so much the poorer the Church.

What is right about the Church, then, is that whatever else it does or does not do, the Church sustains the memory of Jesus with women and always recalls it and has often heeded it, at times in genuinely significant ways.

There are at least six contributions of the Church to Christian feminism that flow from the vision of Jesus. In the first place, the Church has from the earliest times preserved the notion of an alternative life-style for women. The admission of women to recognized religious orders in the Church and the confirmation of the single state as a recognized call from God to women as well as to men has been and continues to be a strong affirmation of the integrity and spirituality of women.

The posture implies that women can receive a call from God that is uniquely theirs and have the soul and the grace and the mind to respond to it.

Women, in other words, do not have to be defined by a man, owned by a man, coupled to a man, identified by a man, or controlled by a man to be a fully adult and right-functioning human being. Women, it seems, are fully rational and equally spiritual beings in their own right. The implications are awesome. If women, like men, can be called alone and separately to God's service, then God's grace is simply not sexist. God's grace simply cannot be trusted to limit itself. But if grace is not gender specific, then God may ask the same things of women that God asks of men, or else it is not the Church which is being held hostage to sexism. It is God who is being held hostage to sexism. God may want absolutely outrageous things of women. God may have absolutely outrageous plans for women. Grace once released is a dangerous thing.

There is a second contribution of the Church to Christian feminism: Consider, too, that female role models have always been defined and upheld in the Church as much models for men, surely, as John and Sebastian and Francis of Assisi, for instance, are for women. All the saints have been given to all the Church for emulation. Sainthood—the fullness of service and the fullness of self—is accepted and applauded and expected of women as well as of men in the church. Teresa of Avila, doctor of the Church, and Catherine of Sienna, counselor of the pope, and Therese of Lisieux, seeker of priesthood, and Joan of Arc, leader of men, and Gertrude and Mechtilde and Hildegarde, abbesses of great dual monasteries, and Hilda, convener of Church synods, and Jane Frances de Chantal, wife and mother with a second career, are indeed holy hopes and worthwhile ideals to be aspired to by women as well as by men.

If the Litany of Saints in the Catholic Church says anything at all, it says that women's lives have made a difference, both to the Church and to the world—a position, incidentally, rarely conceded by other institutions in their history books.

There is a third contribution of the Church to Christian feminism. There is no doubt that the Roman Catholic concept of sacramentality—the notion that divine grace is given without prejudice to sex—marks women as well as men as channels of God's grace. Sacramentality is, therefore, an important contribution to the recognition of the full humanity of women. Why some graces work on women—Baptism, Confirmation, Eucharist, Penance, Sacrament of the Sick and Marriage, for instance—and some do not, why women are impediments to some graces but not to others, is yet to be explained, of course. But there is at least a clearly-developed theology of Baptism, Grace, Incarnation and Redemption that legitimate the question.

Women, it is now argued, can get grace. They simply cannot give it. God's grace goes powerless when it gets to women—blocked apparently by some deficiency of nature—but ironically and gracefully enough, it is the best doctrines of the Church itself which continue to challenge that thought.

There is a fourth contribution that the Church makes to Christian feminism. Feminine spirituality, from the time of the nonviolent Jesus who instructed Peter to put away his sword and the apostles to feed the famished five thousand, continues to mark the Church to our own time.

It is interesting to note that the two more prophetic, more troublesome documents of our own day, the Bishop's Peace Pastoral and the Bishop's Pastoral on the American Economy, are also the most feminine. In a world that calls for power and superiority and control and order and domination and a logical approach to an enemy world, these pastorals call for cooperation and flexibility and support and a feeling of concern for the poor and oppressed. And it is precisely on those grounds that they are being criticized as "foolish" and "incompetent" and "weak" and even "ridiculous." Women have known that kind of criticism for eons.

At the same time, no documents of the American Catholic Church sound more like the Gospel unglossed, unwarped, and undistorted. The Church, it seems, affirms the feminine and needs it for the fullness of the Gospel, and suffers when it realizes that. Strange. Interesting. Disturbing. Hopeful.

There is a fifth contribution of the Church to Christian feminism. Beyond all these other things, there is in the Church a sense of sin, a call to conversion, a consistent reach for reconciliation in the work of righteousness.

Paul confronted Peter for rejecting the vision that lifted Jewish dietary laws from Christianity, and Peter repented. Peter confronted the early Church for rejecting Gentiles in the Jewish Christian community, and the early Church repented. (Acts: 11) Vatican II confronted the contemporary Church with its anti-Semitism and its failure to respond to the Protestant reformers, and the Church is attempting to repent.

If the Church is true to its own best doctrines, and its own best insights, and its own best graces, and its own best definition of Church, and to the vision of Jesus that it preserves, sustains and preaches, it is inevitable that one day it will also confess and repent the sin of sexism.

Finally, there is an overarching contribution of the Church to Christian feminism that defies the diminishment of half of the human race. The image of Mary, the Mother of God, and Mary, the Mother of the Church, is a strong affirmation of the independence, the fullness of grace, and the necessary participation of women in the divine work of salvation.

Some years ago, one of the pillars of Marian piety was a book entitled, *A Woman Wrapped in Silence*. Somehow, in that approach, Mary came across as remote and ethereal, unreal and unreachable. She swept on and off its pages in gossamer and shawl. She was docile and bowed and passive. Strong in suffering, yes, but not like women who had to bend their wits to live and bear and survive. Not like women who gave their entire lives for the salvation of others.

Mary, it seemed, was simply a pawn in the will of God. But a "pawn in the will of God" is a contradiction in terms. There simply cannot be a "pawn in the will of God." The will of God is something that must be chosen and that costs. The will of God is not a trick played on the unsuspecting. The will of God is always an offer of co-creation. Mary was asked, and Mary said Yes.

Mary was a partner in the plan, not a pawn. Mary was free to say no, not enslaved in a pseudo yes. Mary was invited to depart from the system in order to fulfill it. If we understand that, then we begin to understand Mary in a new way. And we also begin to understand the role of women in Church and society in a new way.

It wasn't that Mary was "a woman wrapped in silence." It was simply that her actions spoke more loudly than any number of words could ever do.

We, all of us, women and men, need to understand those actions now. The fact is that Mary is not simply, "Mary, the Mother of God." No, on the contrary. The Mother of God is the image of women everywhere. The Mother of God is Mary, independent woman; Mary, the unmarried mother; Mary, the homeless woman; Mary, the political refugee; Mary, the Third World woman; Mary, the mother of the condemned; Mary, the widow who outlives her child; Mary, the woman of our time who shares in the divine plan of salvation; Mary, the Bearer of Christ.

Mary, you see, could withstand and confront every standard of her synagogue and of her society, and take the poverty and the oppression and the pain to which that led because the will of God meant more to her than the laws of any system. That's the kind of woman God chose to do God's work. That's the kind of woman that the Church raises up for women to be. That's the woman who made the *Magnificat* the national anthem of women everywhere. Indeed, God was with her. And because of Mary, God is also with us. How can we possibly do less?

The Church has preserved the vision of Jesus, and an alternative life-style for women, and the witness of women saints, and the concept of sacramentality, and a consciousness of conversion, and the call to feminine spirituality, and the model of Mary—Mother of God and Mother of the Church. How can we possibly do less?

What is most right about the Church to a feminist is that moment in time when Jesus said, "Woman, you are healed of your infirmity," and straightened to full-size the woman too stooped to stand. And he did it while he was teaching the Torah, in the middle of the synagogue, in the presence of the Pharisees, on a Sabbath, and despite the law.

So to the question, "Why does a woman like you stay in the Catholic Church?," I say, "Precisely because I am Catholic." What is spiritual wisdom? Spiritual wisdom is the ability to recognize the butterfly in a caterpillar; the eagle in an egg; the saint in the sinner.

Are these women trying to destroy the Church?

"I have no idea what tomorrow will bring," the disciple said, "and I don't know how to prepare for it."

"You fear tomorrow," the Holy One said, "not realizing that yesterday is just as dangerous."

It is not on novel doctrine that Christian feminists depend. On the contrary. It is on yesterday's dangerous vision that Christian feminism stakes its hope.

And that is very right.

5

Of Moses' Mother and Pharoah's Daughter: a Model of Contemporary Contemplation

The Talmud instructs, "If you expect to see the final results of your work, you have simply not asked a big enough question."

Well, if the major problem of a meaningless world is narrowness of vision, then our age certainly need not fear. In the lifetime of many of the people still alive, Thomas Merton laid before the world a question the scope of which may well decide its future.

All of his adult life, Thomas Merton struggled, and provoked us to struggle, with the question of contemplation. His biographers record that at various stages of his life, depending on his own circumstances, Merton either made fun of contemplation or lusted after it or argued its meaning or poked at its veneer or wrestled with its demands.

Merton read about contemplation and wrote about contemplation and talked about contemplation everywhere he could. He researched the ancients on it, and moved to the woods to find more of it, and then left the woods both to teach it and to learn it. And, in the end, he went to the East to plumb it, only to discover there that he had already identified it and left it at home.

He said of contemplation: "It is the mark of the true mystic that, after their initiation into the mysteries of the unitive life, they are impelled, in some way, to serve humanity." And in the course of it all, in one of the most chaotic moments of history, Thomas Merton, contemplative, influenced more people than any other religious figure of his time.

He questioned often whether or not his own contemplative order was really contemplative. He struggled to find a balance between contemplation and social activism and most of all, by the honesty of his grappling and the tenterhooks of his very singular, very double, very separated, very involved life, he called the rest of us to contemplation as well.

The question is: What is it to be called to contemplation? And why? And where is such a thing to be found? Well, Merton's call is not a new one. The call to contemplation is, in fact, the basis of every great wisdom of the world.

Contemplation, it seems, is the ability to see through, and to see into, and to see despite and to see without blinders. In America today, perhaps as never before, there is great need for seeing hearts, for contemplative awareness of the kind of world we are creating today for tomorrow. In the United States, there is an awesome kind of blindness in vogue. In this culture, the blind count happiness in things. The American philosophy of happiness, it seems, teaches that life must always be easy, and life must always be comfortable, and life must always be personally fulfilling, and life, at least American life, must always be secure, and life must always look the way we think it should look.

In this world, consequently, it is success, not learning, that has become the goal of education. In America, it is the salary scale rather than the work itself that has become the measure of the job. And money rather than character has become the standard of success. And things rather than values have become the mark of personal achievement. And what we can't take with us rather than what we have left behind so that others can live has become our definition of the quality of life. And what we got for ourselves instead of what we helped to provide for everybody else has become the boast of our ability. And, as a result, pathological individualism and materialism cloud the vision and choke compassion.

And out of that way of seeing, consequently, we have planned the end of the world and we have made it the largest wartime industry of any peacetime world, except proportionally, perhaps, for

Rome whose bloated and extended militarism brought the Empire down. Out of that way of seeing, we have the mentally ill sleeping on the heating grates of our cities and we call it "personal freedom." Out of that way of seeing, we have thousands dying from AIDS and we ignore them in the name of morality. Out of that way of seeing, we have women by the score living in poverty because our welfare programs are designed to punish people who need help rather than to help people whom life has already punished enough, and we justify that sin under the guise of "motivation" or "woman's role." Out of that way of seeing, we have an entire generation of youngsters underfed, undereducated and underdeveloped because we care more about giving money to the contras than we do about providing services for our own children. We spend more on bombs than we do on babies; we allocate more for human destruction than we do for human development. And, oh, yes, our pride is that we are not a welfare state; but we can, apparently, be a warfare state and not even have the grace to blush. Indeed, there is blindness aplenty in us.

And what should we do about it? I suggest that we must begin to struggle, as Merton did, with the difference between complacency and contemplation. We must begin to struggle, as Merton did, with the difference between true and false contemplation. Because indeed there is a contemplation that is for its own sake. This kind of contemplation seeks comfort in prayer and consolation for the spirit and interventions by God to save us from things not created by God, but by ourselves. That kind of contemplation is, at its best, some kind of transcendental complacency that is at least lulling, but probably infantile and certainly unconscionable. That kind of contemplation makes a blessing out of blindness and anoints the unaware who, in the name of Christianity, practice civil religion instead: "My country, right or wrong, but my country"; "America: Love it or leave it"; and who, in the name of citizenship, sell their souls to the separation of conscience from civil life. That kind of contemplation cares more for ritual than for righteousness and maintains law rather than justice.

But there is another kind of contemplation that came to the prophets, but was expected of watchers on the city walls as well. Ezekiel writes: "If someone hears the sound of the horn, but pays no attention, the sword will overtake them and destroy them and they will have been responsible for their own death. If, however, the sentry had seen the sword coming but had not blown the horn and so the people are not alerted and the sword overtakes them and destroys them, the latter shall indeed die. But I will hold the sentry responsible for that death." And then the Scripture reads, "And I have appointed you as sentry . . ." (Ezekiel 33: 1-7).

I have appointed you to contemplate the situation, I have appointed you to search for the truth behind the truth, the whole truth. I have appointed you to see the whole truth, to grasp all of what is there. I have appointed you to be aware. That kind of contemplation is not for its own sake. On the contrary, as the Sufi say, "The candle is not there to illuminate itself."

But where shall we go for a model of that kind of contemplative consciousness, we who often feel more weak than we ever do strong; we who usually feel more alone than part of a rising human consciousness; we who commonly rank ourselves more with the powerless than with the powerful.

I suggest that what the world needs anew is to reflect on the model of contemplation that illuminates the life of two simple women who lived in a world environment not very unlike our own. I suggest as a model of contemporary contemplation the biblical figures of Moses' mother and Pharoah's daughter: Moses' mother and Pharaoh's daughter were two unlikely contemplatives, if ever the world were in search. The Scripture reads:

> Now a certain man of the house of Levi married a Levite woman who conceived and bore a son. Seeing that he was a goodly child, she hid him for three months. When she could hide him no longer, she took a papyrus basket, daubed it with bitumen and pitch and putting the child in it, placed it among the reeds on the river bank. His sister stationed herself at a distance to find out what would happen to him.

Pharaoh's daughter came down to the river to bathe, while her maids walked along the river bank. Noticing the basket among the reeds, she sent her handmaid to fetch it. On opening it, she looked, and lo, there was a baby boy, crying! She was moved with pity for him and said, "It is one of the Hebrews' children." Then his sister asked Pharaoh's daughter, "Shall I go and call one of the Hebrew women to nurse the child for you?" "Yes, do so," she answered. So the maiden went and called the child's own mother. Pharaoh's daughter said to her, "Take this child and nurse it for me, and I will repay you." The woman therefore took the child and nursed it. When the child grew, she brought him to Pharaoh's daughter, who adopted him as her son and called him Moses. (Exodus 2: 1-10)

The implications are clear. Moses' mother was a member of the outcast people. Pharoah's daughter was pure establishment. But both of them had plenty to lose from seeing. Moses' mother, who had nothing, risked the loss of even more; not simply her child's life, but her own life, and the life of her family, and the life of her entire people. They were low class now; to confront the law could only make them even lower. And Pharaoh's daughter? Well, Pharoah's daughter risked the loss of everything, too! Pharoah's daughter risked the loss of status and approval by "the right people" and acceptance by her family and the judgment of orthodoxy. And her future: What would the Pharoah do when he discovered her defiance? What would the people think about her consorting with the enemy? What would the neighbors say about her raising a minority child? How would the government respond to her harboring a refugee?

Here is a situation where the law is very clear that these kinds of people, these foreigners, these defenseless ones are to be controlled because it is good for the government, and it is good for the economy, it is good for all the security and power and affluence we value, that's why! And because it was even good for the Jews themselves, surely, whose role in life, God-given we must obviously presume, was to be slaves. Here in a situation like this, two women defy the political nothingness that being female implied, then, as now, now as then.

Because they saw life differently than did the people around them, two women, one inside an oppressive system and one outside that oppressive system, simply joined hands across national boundaries to subvert a sinful system. Two women are aware of the sinfulness of the system and simply refuse to accept it; two women contemplate a greater good and simply must respond to it; two simple, contemplative women save the Jewish people, not simply Moses.

So why did they do it? And what does their doing have to do with us? The answer, I believe, lies in the nature of contemplation and the nature of the times. The answer lies, I think, in what Merton means when he says, "Contemplation is sudden gift of awareness, an awakening to the real within all that is real." When Moses' mother and Pharaoh's daughter saw the circumstances, suddenly they saw a law above the law, a life above life, an end without end, a sight beyond what was seen. Together, two contemplative women cut through the male system of nationalism and patriarchy and extermination. The Jewess entrusted her baby to the enemy; the Egyptian saw value in the Jew. The kingdom of God became the native country of both. And power came to the powerless to confront the powerful whatever the cost. It was a moment that spoke of the presence of God in life. It was a very contemplative moment.

"Contemplation," Merton wrote, "is the response to a call, a call from the God who has no voice, and who speaks in everything that is, and who, most of all, speaks in the depths of our own being words meant to answer to God, to echo God, and even in some way, to contain God and signify God." Contemplation, in other words, is the ability to see as God sees. Contemplation is the awareness of the divine in the natural. Contemplation is the call to co-creation. And contemplation, therefore, if the model of Moses' mother and Pharaoh's daughter has any meaning at all, must obviously have four dimensions. For contemplation to be real, it must have consciousness, conviction, courage, and constancy.

To see the cosmic sin of the obliteration of the Jewish race in the death of its first-born males was an instance of contemplative consciousness. But contemplation means that consciousness compels. To take the child from the bullrushes and commit oneself not only to save the child but to save the tradition rather than to need to convert or control it, in an act of comtemplative conviction Pharaoh's daughter decides, "Yes, go; get one of his own to nurse him." Contemplation means that consciousness commits. To judge the system and then to fly in the face of the system, as Moses' mother did when she challenged the conscience of one of its own, and as Pharaoh's daughter did when she used her position in behalf of the innocent, is an act of contemplative courage. Contemplation requires that consciousness cry out in witness. To commit themselves to the long-term cost of seeing the vision through, despite the pain and the losses and the dull, dull demands of dailiness, is an act of contemplative constancy. True contemplation, you see, demands that conscience contend to the end.

Contemplation is the ability to see a whole world instead of a partial one. Contemplation is the awareness of the holy in everything. Contemplation is conscience co-creating. The problem is that the people are in peril again and contemplation, it seems, is today at a premium.

Three issues of our time call in a special way for contemplative consciousness: Nuclearism, the notion that massive evil can be permitted in the name of resistance to evil; Globalism, the notion that those who starve in Africa while our barns are full of wheat have claim on our conscience; and Feminism, the notion that women are just as graced and as gracing as men.

The simple truth is that in a world that is linked by a single camera, under the threat of destruction from a single trigger, drawing from a single resource pool, and ruled only by the male model, no one can with integrity ignore the call to contemplate the effects of all of this on creation and our own commitment to it.

We ignore at our peril the biblical frieze of Moses' mother and Pharaoh's daughter who saw their situation, contemplated its implications in the light of eternal truth, confronted the powerful in their sin, cooperated across differences, refused to demonize one another, mentored the next generation in their midst, preserved the enemy and saved the nation.

As sure as the baby in the bullrushes, the signs of the fragility of our own world and the chaos in our own system are everywhere. Women are the poorest of the poor, in this country as well as everywhere in the world, because their work is undervalued, their talents are overlooked, their life development is circumscribed and, right to the end, even when they have done exactly what the system wanted them to do, stay home, raise a family, be a good wife and mother, the system conspires to cheat them out of Social Security monies by giving the widow less than the widower of money that was supposed to have been jointly theirs.

Who can contemplate such a contradiction, who can see with the compassionate eye of God, and do nothing?

Or, imagine in your mind's eye three tin pails. Now in the first tin pail, drop 2 BB's. Those 2 BB's represent the total amount of firepower, including the two atomic bombs, that was used in all of World War II.

Now, go to the second tin pail and, one at a time, slowly, drop into that bucket 32 BB's. Those 32 BB's represent the amount of firepower it would take to unleash nuclear winter on this planet and destroy all life on earth.

Finally, in your mind's eye, stand in front of your third tin pail. Into that pail, slowly, one at a time, drop 2, 32, 100, 1000, 1500, 2000, 2500, 3000, 3500, 4000, 4500, 5000, 5500, 5600, 5700, 5800, 5900, 6000 BB's. Those 6000 BB's represent the total amount of nuclear firepower now existing in American and Soviet arsenals.

And while the poor the world over struggle to eat, and the illiterate struggle to get educated, and families struggle to raise children, and the homeless struggle for their dignity, if not their dreams, the superpowers build and buy five more nuclear bombs each, every single day.

With the factory system what it is, why? With agriculture what it is, why? With the national debt what it is, why?

"Hatred," the philosopher wrote, "is simply a slower form of suicide."

Isn't it time to contemplate what it is that makes our enemies enemies?

And who decided it?

And over what?

One day they told us that the Japanese were fundamentally dishonest and that Germans were essentially cruel. The next day, the Germans and the Japanese became our most important allies and our most ardent supporters.

What happened to the "fundamentals"? Whatever became of the list of "essential elements"? Isn't the "enemy" really only whoever someone else tells us that they are?

Young men die in old men's wars, they say. And that's true. But only after enough brainwashing and enough fear and enough demonizing of the enemy has been done to send German boys against Russian boys unthinkingly, or American boys against Vietnamese boys uncaringly; or Palestinian boys against Israeli boys willingly, with great ideals in mind and the drumbeats of glory in their ears.

The problem is that in a world where every decent thing that humankind has ever done is now in peril, both our future and our past, both Shakespeare and the space shuttle, we may no longer have the luxury of allowing our government to choose our enemies for us. Hate is indeed simply a slower form of suicide, and in our society we are already beginning to feel its atrophying effects.

SDI is already the largest item in the Pentagon budget, while funds for education, and food stamps, and subsidized housing, and day care, all women's issues and children's issues, get smaller everyday.

Who can truly contemplate such a situation, who can see what creation was meant to be but is not, who can see with the compassionate eye of God and say nothing?

A polluted planet, the growing numbers of poor in the Garden of Paradise, the lust for a kind of "progress" that diminishes the prospects of the next generation all cry for contemplative consciousness.

According to World Watch Institute's "State Of The World, 1987," in the tropics, ten trees are being cut for every one tree planted. As a result, forests are shrinking at a fairly predictable rate. Large-scale depletion of the ozone shield and the development of chlorofluorocarbons, population concentration and the overtaxing of local water sources, fuel supplies and disposal capacities all bring into relief the fact that the very notion of "progress" is ripe for redefinition.

Who can contemplate poverty in affluence, power for profit, women, as a class, in oblivion throughout the world, or prejudices enthroned as morality? Who can contemplate all this with the compassionate eye of God and do nothing, say nothing, change nothing, stand for nothing?

But contemplation is not without cost. To see what should be instead of what is; to see what could be instead of what will be if things go on as they are; to see what is possible instead of what is probable; to be conscious and compassionate and courageous and constant about it, costs.

"The duty of the contemplative life," Merton wrote, "is to provide an area in which possibilities are allowed to surface and new choices beyond routine choice become manifest.

Contemplative time," he went on, "is compassionate time; contemplative time is time open to others."

But to do the civil disobedience, the "citizen diplomacy," the act of conscience of Moses' mother and Pharoah's daughter, to cry out like the sentry in the night, takes its toll. But once we begin to see, what other choice is there? Once we become seeing souls, how can we not? An Arab proverb reminds us, "I will set my face to the wind and scatter my handful of seeds. It is no big thing to scatter seeds, but I must have the courage to keep facing the wind."

Yet in the midst of all the effort that consciousness, conviction, courage and constancy take to become compassion, the monastic literature of the ancients show us clearly what it takes to rise to heights of contemplative awareness.

The story is told that a young person once came to the monastery disillusioned with life but wanting to find a short cut to enlightenment, for fear that a hard, slow process of study and meditation would only lead to failure. And so the Elder said: "Ah, yes, there is a shorter way to enlightenment. I will put you to playing chess with one of our old sisters. Whichever one of you loses, I will cut off your head. If the old sister loses, she will wake up in Paradise. If you lose, since you have done nothing so far with your life, you will simply deserve it."

When the game began, the youth played for her life. The chessboard became her entire world; she was totally concentrated on it. And though the early stages of the game were a near equal struggle, the youth finally took the advantage and the old sister's position began to crumble. And then the young person saw the worn face of her opponent and its intelligence and its sincerity, and a wave of compassion came over her. And deliberately she began to make one blunder after another in her opponent's behalf until finally her own position was completely defenseless. And then the master leaned forward and upset the board. "There is no winner and no loser," the Elder said. "There is no head to fall here."

"Life requires of us only two things," the elder said to the youth, "concentration on what is important and compassion for the other, and you have just learned both. Pursue that spirit and your enlightenment is sure."

That's the kind of contemplation that put Moses in the river and that's the kind of contemplation that took him out. And that's the kind of contemplation for which Merton called. And that's the only kind of contemplation with its consciousness and conviction and courage and constancy that will preserve this planet and its peoples in our own time.

That's the awareness, that's the insight, that's the call to alarm, that's the kind of contemplation that must grow in our lives. And it is, I believe, that kind of contemplative consciousness to which Moses' mother and Pharaoh's daughter in this time call us all.

Why?

Because there truth is alive; there all creation is one; and there God's face shines, as it should, in us.

6

Spirituality and Contemporary Culture

Somewhere there reads the following definition of an American: "Americans are people who are born in the country, where they work with great energy so they can live in the city, where they work with even greater energy so that someday they can live in the country again." Right or wrong, the definition has a great deal to say about the relationship between culture and spirituality—about what you do with what you are—and why you do it.

Two pieces of religious literature indicate with special clarity the essential connectedness of spiritual maturity and cultural consciousness. The first comes from Exodus 3:18. "On Horeb," the Scripture tells, "the angel of Yahweh appeared to Moses in the shape of a flame of fire, coming from the middle of a bush. There was the bush, blazing, but it was not being burnt up, 'I must go and look at this strange sight,' Moses said, 'and see why the bush is not burnt.' Now Yahweh saw him go forward to look and God called to him from the middle of the bush. 'Moses,' he said, 'come no nearer. Take off your shoes, for the place where you are is holy ground.' And then Yahweh said, 'I have seen the miserable state of my people in Egypt. I have heard their appeal to be free. I am well aware of their sufferings. I mean to deliver them. So, I'm sending you to Pharoah to bring my people out . . . .' "

The message is a dramatic one. Just at what would seem to be the moment of Moses' total immersion in the presence of God, God stops Moses where Moses is to teach him that his holiness depends on finding holiness where he stands and then by taking that energy to other people for their liberation. Moses learns that holiness is made of virtues, not of visions; Moses learns that holiness depends on being for the other; Moses learns that holiness depends on being about something greater than the self; Moses learns that holiness is being present to the presence everywhere it is and even where it seems it isn't.

The second story of culture and spirituality comes from the tales of the Hasidim. An old rabbi of great wisdom, whose fame had spread beyond his own congregation to villages and rabbis far on the other side of the mountains, one day, suddenly, died. The young rabbis were bereft. "Now," they said, "what shall we do when our people look to us for guidance? Without the old master, where shall we get the answers to the great questions of life?" So they decided among themselves to pray and fast until the old man's holiness and wisdom would be infused into one of them. And sure enough, one night in a dream, the old man appeared to one of the younger rabbis. "Master," the young teacher said, "it is good that you have returned. Now, with you gone, the people look to us for answers to the great questions of life and we are still unsure. For instance, Master, they demand to know 'On the other side, of what account are the sins of youth?'" "The sins of youth?" the old man asked. "Why, on the other side the sins of youth are of no account whatsoever." And the young rabbi said, "On the other side the sins of youth are of no account whatsoever? Then, what has it all been about? On the other side, what sin is punished, if not the sins of youth?" And the old man answered slowly and clearly, "On the other side, that sin which is punished with constant and unending severity is the sin of false piety."

The point is clear: Piety is cultural. Holiness depends on our choosing the pieties proper to the times. Culture and spirituality, in other words, are of a piece. As Moses and the old master both knew, the function of spirituality is not to protect us from our times; the function of spirituality is to enable us to leaven it, and stretch it, and bless it, and break it open to the present will of God.

And what does all of that mean to the retreat movement? Well, if culture is the way people think and feel and behave as a people, and spirituality is the way we live out the life and teachings of Jesus in this particular culture, at this particular time, then the question for retreat directors must become: What cultural realities are challenging the Gospel now, and how can the Gospel best challenge the culture if we, here, now, are really to be a holy people? The history of spirituality identifies three basic responses to culture: the intellectual, the relational, and the performative.

An *intellectual spirituality* the scholars define as a spiritual life that is creed-centered and concerned with beliefs and committed to union with God. An intellectualist spirituality is good at drawing denominational lines and identifying heretics and maintaining orthodoxy and having personal mystical experiences. The intellectualist wants to stay and contemplate the bush.

A *relational spirituality* is committed to the development of human bondedness as the preeminent model of the Christian life. The relationalist talks a lot about love and the relationalist is willing to stay in Egypt if necessary, bush or no bush, to keep the slaves company in their pain.

Finally, *performative spirituality* is action-centered. Performers in the spiritual life are "Our Father" people. They pray every day, "Thy kingdom come, Thy will be done" and then they do something to bring it. Performers are people who know that the word is incomplete until it has become transforming action. Performers would prefer to reform Egypt—by carrying the burning bush back there.

The question for us is, what is our cultural situation now? And which type of spirituality is most needed and how do we build it and what does that have to do with retreat centers?

Let's look briefly at the cultural situation in the United States from 1960-1988, the era that has formed the spiritual life of most of us. In this period, we have experienced major shifts in the national belief-value system. Family patterns have changed, sex roles have changed, and governments that talked freedom and justice and human rights have been riven with one corruption after another and so became daily less and less credible. The most dramatic transformation of world view that ever took place in human history has taken place in this period. John Glenn, first American astronaut, took, from outer space, the only picture of the planet that had ever been taken. And he took it with a $45.00 camera that he bought at the local drugstore just before the trip. Up until that moment, the human view of earth and its place in the universe had never been anything else but theory and speculation and educated calculations. Up until that moment, you and I knew where we lived only on the basis of artistic guesses. Now, for the first time in history, we could really see ourselves in all our grandeur—and in all our smallness.

This generation, too, saw scientific progress that was often more threat than help. In these few years, science changed life, changed death, changed family, changed sex, changed birth. And changed war from struggle to annihilation. Until, finally, science has managed, in our generation, to change the very meaning of "meaning." In this era, military security became our highest priority, our greatest expenditure, and our scarcest commodity. Thanks to our "military security," indeed, we have created the end of the world and we are storing it in the cornfields of Kansas.

In this age, too, we have seen new interest in the wisdom of the East as the wealth of the West lost its power to save. American dominance, isolation and perfect security ended with the launching of Sputnik. And the rise of a Third World, with its commitment to neutrality, challenged the U.S. notion of its "Manifest Destiny," To be the "city on the hill," "the new Eden," "the covenanted people," as never before in U.S. history.

In this same time frame, integration challenged white supremacy. And feminism challenged the white male system and even the white male god. And great poverty in the midst of great affluence— the working poor—this very moment challenges all the American myths ever made about fair play, and blessing and the Protestant ethic and the American dream and freedom and justice for all.

And all of this has happened in a society where 10% of the world—Western Europeans and North Americans—consume, hoard, waste or control two-thirds of the resources of the world. Indeed, social consensus on values and beliefs has broken down. The annual survey of college freshmen, sponsored by the American Council on Education and the University of California, finds in the midst of all of this that, unlike their predecessors, this year's college freshmen are less concerned about pollution, more approving of abortion, less opposed to the death penalty, more intent on cohabitation before marriage, less committed to the elimination of racism, less obligated to help others in difficulty, less interested in environmental clean-up and control, considerably less concerned about developing a philosophy of life, and extremely more interested in being "very well off financially."

And all of this while the government spent only $0.20 of every disposable dollar, minus entitlements, in 1987 on human resources—education, employment, job training, social services, health, and fiscal assistance—but spent $0.64 of every tax dollar Congress has the authority to distribute on the military.

Indeed, we need spiritual-cultural revitalization. Indeed, the consensus of old values has broken down. Indeed, the spirit is dying in the most church-going nation in the world. Indeed, the current spiritual-cultural dilemma looms large. Individualism infects every institution; individualism has been raised to the point of high art; individualism erases the Trinitarian model of life in common; individualism runs rampant—to the point of the pathological—in this society at a time, in fact, when global community is urgent if both this planet and its peoples are to be saved.

Our current spiritual dilemma, then, lies in how to link the personal with the public dimensions of life; how to make private spirituality the stuff of public leaven in a world fiercely private and dangerously public at the same time. The fact is that simple spiritualities of creed and community and cooperation are no longer enough. We need now, surely, a spirituality of contemplative co-creation if the culture is to be Christianized. No—if Christians are to be Christianized. Genesis insists that the function of humanity is to nurture and cultivate and care and procreate and have dominion over. Carrying on God's work in the world is, in other words, "the spiritual life."

And what does religion and the retreat movement have to do with all of that? When culture is in chaos and society is in upheaval, it may be important to look for a moment at the process of social revitalization. The anthropologist Anthony F.C. Wallace teaches that major transformations of thought and behavior happen in a society when society discovers that a common set of religious understandings have become impossible to sustain. At that point, Wallace says, the society begins to undergo a "revitalization movement" of four major stages.

Stage one is a period of serious individual stress. In this stage, people begin to question past values and start to establish new patterns of thought and behaviors. They don't think about things as they once thought about things. What the generation before them took for granted, they begin to debate and discard.

In stage two, wide-reaching social stress becomes apparent. What we once called our culture is now barely recognizable, and people begin to decide that their problems aren't personal. Their problems, they decide, are a result of failure in the anchor institutions they had depended on for stability and direction. The churches are out of tune with their need; the schools remote from their life questions; the government corrupt and corrupting. There is political rebellion in the streets, and schism in the churches.

In stage three, though people as a whole recognize a problem, they can't agree on how to cope with this new social situation. Some want to change the system; some want to send in the troops. And they quarrel and divide and blame authority.

Then, inevitably, in stage three of a revitalization movement, a nativist or traditionalist movement arises. Nativists argue that the danger has come from the failure of the people to adhere more strictly to old beliefs and values and behavior patterns. They want the "old time religion," and they find scapegoats aplenty. The economy would be all right if it weren't for unions; marriages would be all right if it weren't for feminism, and the country would be fine if it weren't for communism.

In the fourth, and final, stage of a revitalization movement, Wallace points out, comes the building of a new worldview and the restructuring of old institutions to enable it. In simpler societies, the leadership for this rebuilding of the society usually came from a single charismatic person. "And Moses intervened," Psalm 89 reminds us, "and you, O God, turned aside your destruction." In more complex cultures, like our own, multiple spokespersons are needed to lead the people to new understandings about old values. The role of these spiritual leaders is not to repudiate the older worldview entirely, but to shed new light on it so that it can be remembered that God's spirit manifests itself always in new ways to meet new needs. Then, more flexible people begin to understand and experiment with the new consensus so that cultural transformation—the movement from death to life—of an entire people begins to happen.

Finally, not the older generation, not the sojourners who brought old ideas and goals and values and designs from one desert to another with them, but the generation that "grew up with" the emerging insights, the generation that spent their life wandering in the desert and knew no other, comes to maturity. And old institutions find themselves with new leadership. And the institutions are restructured, provided that someone brings them up with the new questions and the new insights.

And how do we know it can happen? Because in this country alone we have seen one generation withdraw their allegiance to a king, and the next abolish slavery, and the one after that regulate businesses, and the last empower laborers and this one, now, here, beginning to struggle for liberation and equality and survival. "And Moses intervened," the Psalm teaches, "and you turned aside your destruction." What God saves, in other words, God saves through us. Just as God did with Sodom and Gomorrah and Mordechai and Esther and Isaac and Jacob and Joseph and the Pharoah and every requester of miracles in the New Testament.

We need to intervene for one another. We need a new world view that puts the old one "in new light." But how? And where will this "spirituality of contemplative co-creation" come from in an individualistic culture? And in what way can the religious leaders of our time help to build this bridge from privatized piety to public moral responsibility? I suggest that, as directors, we begin to look at the bases of social brokenness; that we ourselves begin to see the spiritual link between the personal and the political. I'm suggesting that retreat houses build programs that look again at the seven capital sins, but this time on two, rather than on simply one, level. The level of the personal, yes. But the level of the global as well.

Envy on the personal level is certainly a lack of acceptance of self which leads in its sinful form to a rejection of others. But at the global level, isn't it ethnocentrism as well? When we uphold criminal governments for our own good rather than recognize the needs of the people of the country, when we impose our values and structures in return for trade, isn't that a form of envy and its failure to accept a thing for what it is?

Pride is, of course, the need to dominate and coerce others on the personal level. But on the global level, isn't it also the mania for national superiority, for being numero uno, for having the best of everything?

Lust is clearly the exploitation of another for the sake of physical satisfaction. We are beginning to recognize it when it's date rape or pornography or selfish sensuality, true, but is there yet enough conscience in us also to see lust as the national passion for the instantaneous gratification that justifies the exploitation of whole peoples so that we can have the cheap cash crops and conveniences we demand that rape their lands and loot their futures? Isn't it the exploitation that comes from lust that leads to the feminization of poverty and the loss of feminine resources and values in a world that is reeling from the institutionalization of masculine values?

Gluttony, the overconsumption of food, leads to waste and bloatedness and misuse of resources on the personal level. But it is also surely at the base of the lack of distribution of surplus to the dying in Ethiopia and the farmers in the Soviet Union. Someone wrote of this culture, "We do not have a war on poverty; we have a war on poor people." And what are we Christians doing about it as we give our retreats?

We speak of covetousness as a lack of a sense of "enough," and we know that on the personal level that leads to the sinful brink of hoarding or an inordinate desire for unnecessary possessions. But what is the difference between that kind of covetousness and the demon that fuels a suicidal arms race in the quest for superiority?

Anger we recognize as the cultivation of an eschatological sense of righteousness and judgment, of putting ourselves in the place of the patient justice of God. And we teach with conviction about the danger of assuming the right to convict and punish the other. "Vengeance is mine; I will repay," we remind one another. But what has happened to the national moral fiber when whatever evil we say of the Soviet Union is counted as virtue; what about the sin of demonizing our enemies, or our refusal to sign the Geneva arms accord agreements or our inability as a nation to hear the other meaning of "human rights"?

We abhor sloth, in its assumption that anyone has the right to live off the efforts of others, in its laziness and lack of responsibility. But where is Christian leadership in the building of a new world view about the sinfulness of multi-national structures which live off the backs of the poor or give unjust wages and benefits or take the unequal treatment of women for granted, and absorb women's lives at lesser pay for the convenience of others, and then moralize about that kind of domestic servitude? And all in the name of "God's will" for us.

And we go on blindly in our search for goodness. We collect garbage to keep our yards clean, not because the earth was not made to absorb those materials. We turn down the heat to save money, not resources. We car pool because of lack of parking spaces, rather than a lack of personal need or a chance to help another. We counsel and educate for individuality and autonomy and control and independence and security and suicidal defense in a world that needs community and mutuality and cooperation and interdependence and human responsibility and contemplative co-creation. We build small shelters for the homeless and huge rockets to make people homeless. And we go to church. And we go to church. And we go to church.

Yet 70% of the respondents to a survey conducted by the Williamsburg Charter Foundation, a non-sectarian organization concerned with religion in U.S. public life, said in January 1988, that "It is important that the president have strong religious beliefs" and that religion has a place in public life. Well, where is that public religion in private life supposed to come from if not from the leaders of the retreat movement? When Jacob saw Joseph in Egypt, he said, "Now that I know that you live, I can die." And God said to Moses, "Stay where you are. Where you are is holy ground."

Clearly, the role of the spiritual life today is, like Jacob, not to die until we have assured a dynamic and meaningful spirituality for the next generation. It is, like Moses, to recognize where we are as the ground of God's grace. It is certainly to enable us to see life differently so that God's reign can happen in our time.

7

Ministering to the Wounded World

There are three stories, I believe, that show us how ministry must differ from mere professional service at this moment in history if our ministries are, indeed, to be real and effective and Gospel and true. The first story comes from the ancient Sufi. Once upon a time, the story goes, a seeker went from land to land to discover an authentic religion. Finally the seeker found a group of extraordinary fame. They were known for the goodness of their lives and they were known for the singleness of their hearts and they were known for the sincerity of their service. "I see all of that," the seeker said, "and I'm impressed by it. But, before I become your disciple, I have a question to ask: Does your God work miracles?" And the disciple said thoughtfully, "Well, it all depends on what you mean by a miracle. Some people call it a miracle when God does the will of people. We call it a miracle when people do the will of God."

The second story comes from the writings of the Hasidim. Once upon a time, the story goes, some disciples begged a rabbi for a word of wisdom to guide them all through life. And though it was the rabbi's day of silence and reflection, he nodded kindly, took a sheet of paper and wrote upon it one single word: "AWARENESS." But the disciples were deeply perplexed. "Rabbi," they said, "that's very brief. Could you please expand on that idea a little?" So the rabbi took the paper back and this time he wrote three words: "Awareness. Awareness. Awareness." And that only confounded the disciples totally. "Tell us what those words mean!" they insisted. So, finally, the elder looked up from the paper and said, "When I say, 'Awareness, awareness, awareness,' I mean awareness!"

The wisdom of the ancients is as clear and as valid as ever. If we really want to minister to the wounded in this world, we are going to have to concentrate, you and I, on developing real religious awareness and on working a few miracles of our own. There are bureaucratic services aplenty in this world. What we really need are ministers. The question is, where shall we go to determine how to minister to the marginalized poor, the disinterested parishioner, the alienated prisoner, the depressed elderly, the invisible woman, the displaced worker, the frightened patient, the bereft family of the dying that is beyond the good word, the warm smile, the caring call, the ministerial glad hand?

What can we do in our time that exceeds the "Be well, stay warm and well fed" mentality that Paul warns about and that the wounded have learned to ignore? How shall we minister, in other words, in ways that change people's lives as much as they warm their environment? How shall we minister, too, in ways that change our own lives, in this vast and deadening world, from the ranks of the burned-out humdrum to the steady, steady godliness of the Gospel?

The answer, I think, lies in a third story, this one from a Scripture that is often translated as a glimpse of glory or a case for contemplative withdrawal from the chaos around us, but which, I believe, is really an insight into the dynamism of dailiness, a call to courage, and a mandate to ministry.

The story that really makes the difference for us in ministry today, I think, is the story of the Transfiguration. The story of the Transfiguration is a journey into ministry with all its misconceptions and all its misunderstandings and all its mistakes and all its mighty power. Mount Tabor, the site of the Transfiguration, is one of those places that is not "on the way" to anywhere. It is steep and rugged and hard to scale. The path that leads to the top of the mountain is hand-hewn out of rock. It is also narrow and dangerous and long. Then, at the top, with the exception of the view of the vast, unending plain of Jezreel, there is nothing there. It's an out-of-the-way place that has all the character of a dead end, a beautiful dead end, true, but a dead end nevertheless.

And it is Tabor to which Jesus took Peter, James and John. But all we have to do is to look at Peter, James and John on Tabor and we will understand, I think, precisely what ministry is all about. In the first place, Peter, James and John thought they had been called to go up the mountain to be with Jesus alone. So, the Scripture says, "They left the world below and went off by themselves," prepared, apparently, to follow Jesus and find God. Mountains, to the ancients, remember, were always points of contact with God since they were the places where earth touched heaven. To go "up to a high mountain" in Jewish spiritual literature, then, is always to be seeking a very special relationship with God. On this particular excursion up the mountain, too, theirs was a very select group. No one else was with them and they had Jesus all to themselves.

And, sure enough, Scripture records that a strange and a wonderful thing occurred there. Up on the top of that faraway mountain, Peter, James and John got a new insight into Jesus. Up there, by themselves, they began to see Jesus differently. He was a great deal more than they had ever imagined. He was as dazzling as the sun and as intense and as all-consuming.

The idea was overwhelming. And very, very heady. And very, very disturbing. Because, then and there, in a Gospel that is apparently about the mystical dimension of the life of Jesus, we begin to see the perennial struggle between piety and Christianity, between comfort and compassion, between social service and ministry, between the barely therapeutic and the deeply healing, between religion-for-real and religion-for-show. There, on the top of the mountain, right in front of their eyes, Jesus, the Scripture says, became transfigured before them, radiant as the sun and talking to Moses and Elijah.

And there's the story that makes the difference. Why? Well, if we're going to see ministry to the wounded as our own task at this time in history, then it's important to realize four things about this Gospel. In the first place, Peter opted for piety. "Jesus, it's good for us to be here," Peter said. "Let's build three booths . . ." After all, Peter knows a good thing when he sees it and Peter plans to settle down here. At the very moment of his deepest revelation and clearest call, in other words, Peter decides that the spiritual life has something to do with building temples and enlarging the office and saying poetic prayers and floating above the fray. After all, the company is choice and the office is comfortable and the environment is nothing if not rarified. Ah, yes, if there is a temptation in Christian ministry today, it is probably the temptation to play church. And therein lies the almost cacophonous cry of this Scripture. No sooner has Peter decided to be a church bureaucrat, a weekday mystic, an office manager than look what happens: Scripture dashes the entire thought in mid-air. "While he was still speaking," the Scripture records, "the voice of God said, 'This is my son . . . Listen!'" And then, the passage continues, Jesus laid his hands on them and said, very simply, very directly, "Get up and do not be afraid." Then, slowly but surely, he began to lead them around the edges of the cliffs, over the rocky road, back down the mountain to the very bottom of the hill to the dirty towns and hurting people and unbelieving officials and ineffective institutions below.

Why?! Because Jesus didn't appear to Peter, James and John with David, the king, or with Aaron, the priest; Jesus didn't show himself to the disciples with those who interpreted the law or defended the country. Jesus didn't reveal his work as either royalty or ritual. No, Jesus identified himself on Tabor with Moses and Elijah; with Moses who had led the people out of oppression, and with Elijah who was known to King Ahab as "The Troubler of Israel," the one who condemned the compromise between true and false gods, the one, in other words, who exposed to the people the underlying causes of their problems. Jesus, the healer, identified himself, not with the kings and the priests of Israel who had maintained its establishments and developed its institutions, good as they were; no, Jesus the healer identified himself with the prophets, with those who had been sent to warn Israel of its unconscionable abandonment of the covenant. Surely there isn't a minister alive today who doesn't understand the pain and the power of this Gospel because this Gospel is the very bedrock lesson of ministry.

If ministry is to have any meaning whatsoever in our times, then we will have to wade into the throngs of hurting people on every plain of this planet, listening, listening, listening to the prophet-healer, Jesus, and exposing to people the underlying causes of all the wounding in this world. And all of that in the face of those in-stitution-types for whom saving the system is much too often a higher priority than saving the people. Of course, spiritual gifting presupposes a long, long journey up a mountain to find God. But the call to ministry also means that you and I simply cannot build a spiritual life and expect to be able to stay on the top of the mountain.

The call of the spiritual life, then, the call of ministry, is the call to take all the insights into the life of Christ that we have ever been able to gather back down the mountain to the world of our own time. The call to ministry in this century is the call to be aware of the root causes of suffering in this world and to work a few miracles of our own.

We work with poor women and battered women and under-nourished women every day and we do that very well, but how can we possibly say that we really minister to women and do nothing about the fact that women get paid less than men for the very same work, or that women seldom get promoted to top management positions, or minister to women with integrity in institutions that say that a married man can be ordained a deacon but a married woman cannot, or that an 11-year-old boy can carry cruets to the altar without bringing the Church to perdition, but an 11-year-old girl cannot, or that God can be called "rock" and "light" and "wind" and "pelican" but never "mother," if we ourselves say nothing to the contrary.

We minister to the hungry and the unemployed and the depress-ed every day and we do that very well, but how can we say that we really minister to the poor if we never so much as question the fact that we are putting more money into weapons of destruction in this country than we are putting into works of development? Or let's put it this way: If you were to count one trillion one dollar bills, one per second, for 24 hours a day, it would take you 32 years to finish counting. But with that $1 trillion, you could buy a $100,000 house for every family in Kansas, Missouri, Nebraska, Oklahoma and Iowa and you could put a $10,000 car in the garage of each one of those houses. And there would be enough money left to build 250 $10 million libraries and 250 $10 million hospitals for every city in those states. And after that, there would still be enough money left over to put in the bank and, from the interest alone, pay 10,000 nurses and 10,000 teachers and still give a $5000 bonus to every family in those five states.

That's what one trillion dollars will buy in this country today. But Star Wars, a death star weapon being sold as a defense system, which most credible scientists say can't possibly work, now while we sit here already carries a price tag of three trillion dollars. How can we possibly say that we're doing enough to minister to the homeless and the poor and the uneducated and the ill and the emotionally stressed, in other words, and never do a thing to try to stop what is eating out the very heart of the country and eroding our social systems and numbing our consciences?

We minister to hurting families by listening and caring and planning and we do all of that very well, but how can we see families on the verge of collapse because their finances are on the verge of collapse, and never say a word about the national debt or the loss of our industries and say we're doing all we can for the hurting families we see?

We minister with warmth and care to the drug addicts and the deprived and the illiterate who wind up in our prisons, and we do that very well, but how can we say we're prison chaplains and do nothing to promote the rehabilitation of the prison system itself?

We minister to the traumatized and the homesick and the frightened in our armed forces with affection and presence and parental concern, and we do that very well, but how can we minister to men and women in the armed forces, tell them that we care about them and that love is the only Christian imperative, and never ourselves say a thing about the immorality of nuclear war or the nuclear policies and the nuclear mentalities that make nuclearism possible? How can we lay the morality of nuclearism and the preservation of the planet on the conscientious objection of 19-year-olds and never even have the grace to blush?

We minister to the angry and the depressed and the despairing with consistency and Christian hope and we do that very well, but how can we call ourselves therapists and never speak out about the national demonizing that's been done to create the enemy it takes to justify the continuation of a wartime economy in peacetime?

We stand for life and human development by being with people in pain, and we do that very well, but how can we cry and cry and cry about abortion, as if it were a single-issue subject, but say nothing about the parental role of men or the equality of women or the deterioration of education or the lack of day-care programs or the planned destruction of the planet that wrings life out of people after birth an inch at a time and say that ministry is our passion?

Almost half of the young adults in this country owned their own homes in 1979. By 1987, that figure was reduced to barely a third, thanks to rising costs and reduced incomes, and rising national debt and the loss of jobs to cheaper markets. But we are trying to care for families, and the country, and the next generation whose opportunities, nevertheless, will be slimmer than ours were and whose horizons will be narrower than ours were because they'll be paying our debts and bearing the burdens of our devotion to the forces of death and destruction for decades.

And who will have ministered to that? And in who of us will they have seen a different story? The Transfiguration, you see, is about more than what happens on the mountain, though go to the mountain every minister must, if only to see for ourselves and to become what we can become and to get a view of the people on the plain below through the eyes of Jesus. People can pay for service and many people do. But ministry, real ministry, is priceless. And can be done only in the name of Jesus. Service is a teachable skill. Ministry is a mark of Elijah, who resisted the government to reveal the true God, and of Moses, who resisted the people to reveal the law of God, and of Jesus, the healing prophet, the prophet healer who demanded more from the disciples than personal faith alone. Jesus demanded commitment to the kingdom from the rich young man; from the disciples; from those who cried out, "Lord, Lord . . ."; from those who blessed the woman who bore him without doing the will of the One who sent him.

Indeed, the problem with the story of the Transfiguration is, you see, that it has two parts. And it is the second part that is, as it was for the apostles, the real measure of ministry. The fact is that when Jesus and the disciples came down from the Mount of Transfiguration, suffering people in droves were waiting for Jesus below. And the Scripture is quite clear why. "I have brought my son to you because he is possessed by a mute spirit, a demon . . . . I asked your disciples to expel him, but they were unable to do so." And the disciples began to ask him privately, "Why is it that we could not expel it?" And Jesus told them, "This kind is driven out only by prayer." This kind is driven out only by insight, not by technique. This kind is driven out only by putting on the mind of Christ, not by putting on more titles or credits or offices. This kind is driven out only by vision, only by risk, only by courage, only by a care that supercedes cost, only by a heart devoted to causes rather than to symptoms. This kind is driven out only by the spirit of Moses and Elijah, whom kings expelled and professionals despised, but to whom the people looked for truth.

Here at the bottom of the mountain, people look to us now to bring the truth, to be the vision, to expel the demons. We live in an information culture now, the analysts tell us, where change is as rapid as the communications system that transmits it. The question is, who will evaluate the changes and critique the consequences of each on the human spirit, if not those who minister to the spirits that are being broken? We live in a high-tech culture which needs desperately to compensate for the impersonalism of technology by the rediscovery of human values. The question is, who will call a world on the brink of death by self-destruction to the cry of human community, if not those who are wearing themselves out ministering to the farmers and children and ill and elderly who are already being denied the fullness of life by a society more given to the technology of death? We live in a culture where industry is fast moving to the Third World. The question is, who will call for building bridges across our cultural differences instead of building fences around our borders, so that by developing others we may also develop ourselves?

We live in a world where short-term advantage must give way to long-term planning and concern for consequences, before pollution and quarterly profit make the planet an afterthought. The question is, who will call the world to care about the future if not those of you who are already ministering to the refugees that profiteering has already made? We live in a world centralized by satellite communication. The question is, who will teach us to think globally and act locally so that the whole world will be a better place to live? Participation has become the order of the day. Every group and people and place, no matter how small, wants to be a part of the process of arriving at decisions that affect their lives. The question is, who will help people to help themselves if not those who minister to the needy?

We live in a world where information is toppling the old pyramids of inherited power. Institutions and hierarchies have failed to solve society's problems and people are beginning to rise up together, in the women's movement and the peace movement and the save-the-whales movement, to do it themselves. The question is, who will help the people at the foot of the mountain to turn the transfiguring light of life into all its other dark spots, if not those who minister, as you do, day and night, night and day, to those made helpless by the system? We live in a world with a shifting economic center that is leaving in its wake a whole new world of poverty and unemployment and undersubsidized public services that breed crime and destitution and ignorance and malnutrition and underdevelopment and revolutionary anger. The question is, who will care for the people left behind? Who will set out to reform the system, if not you who minister firsthand to the results of its wreckage?

Those are the demons of our society. Those are the things being brought this time to us for healing. Indeed, you and I need trans-figuration now. We're ministering in parishes well, but now we must transform the parishes from islands of ritual to arenas of par-ticipation. We're ministering in prisons well, but now we must transform the prisons from places of punishment to centers of new-found dignity. We're ministering to neglected women well, but now we must enable women to find the fullness of humanity, not simply a hard-won faith. We're ministering at bedsides well, but now we must bring the ill and the dying a hope of their importance in our national agenda and attention to the cost of their care, not simply the warmth of our presence. We must be for the poor not simply a handout but a voice in their behalf, where the poor are not heard and their pain is not registered.

If we are really to minister, it is up to us to be transformed and then transfiguring. We must be aware not simply of the pain but we must be aware, as well, of why the hurting hurt. And then we must set out to do something to cure the causes as well as soothe the symptoms. Those are things of which we must be aware if we are to be authentic.

And, if we are really to minister to a wounded world, those are the miracles that you and I must now begin to work. And when they say that's not our role, we must remember that Jesus appeared with Elijah. Our ministry is to continue the work not only of Jesus, the healer, but also of Jesus, the prophet. And when we're tempted to think that we're already too busy doing so much good to do any-thing more, we must remember Jesus wading into the crowd below. Our ministry must be not only to comfort but to challenge; not just to attend to, but also to advocate; not just of vision, but of voice; not only to care, but to change.

The desert monastics tell the story of ministry this way. Past a seeker on a prayer run came the cripple and the beggar and the beaten. And seeing them, the seeker went down, down, down into deep prayer and cried, "Great God! How is it that a loving creator can see such things and yet do nothing about them?" And out of the long, long silence, God said, "I did do something about them. I made you." What does it mean to minister today? It means awareness, authenticity, and transfiguration, transfiguration, transfiguration. I pray for awareness, authenticity, transfiguration, for us all, for their sake and for ours.

8

Formation for Ministry

The problem with our time, the sage wrote, is that the future is not what it used to be. And for religious life, at least, a more real insight has never been divined. The process of past changes in post-Vatican II religious communities has now, it seems, been carefully and clearly described. History will not want for explanations of why change happened or how change happened or that change happened. Our historical debt to the generations that succeed us has been well paid. Sociologists and anthropologists and psychologists and theologians and historians and religious who left their communities and religious who stayed in them through the tumult and transition have all added their analyses to the academic question of how a subculture of grand proportion managed first to petrify and then to thaw.

The question now, then, is not: will religious life change? The question now is: will religious life survive? The question of what we shall renew is well behind us. The question of what we renewed for, however, may well be before us still. Yet, at the very same time that ancient or large or traditional religious orders are struggling to renew and survive, new communities are springing up everywhere—charismatic communities, peace communities, and resistance communities, both Catholic and non-Catholic.

To talk about formation and selection, then, in a time such as ours, when the past is well over and the future is yet unclear, is no small task. If we are not forming for the past and the future is yet unknown, how is either formation or the selection of members possible? What are we forming for? And is there anyone to form? With steadily declining membership in convents and monasteries the world over, is there a future for community life at all? Is the vocation crisis a lack of vocations or a signal of confusion or a sign of new things to come?

The purpose of this article is to explore the present impulses for renewal and direction in religious communities themselves as the prototype of religious organization, and then to apply the experiences and questions of these groups to forms of Christian community that are still in their earliest stages.

The Question of Significance and Spirituality

Given the number of young people who have spent themselves unstintingly in poverty programs and missionary activities and international development programs and the peace movement around the world, it is clear that the youth of our time are as idealistic and as generous as were young people of the past. Given the numbers who line up in droves for wars and money and education and challenge, not all of which are comfortable and most of which demand risk and sacrifice and self-giving, it is hard to say that they are less motivated than the youth before them. If Gospel life in community does not thrive, then, the deficit, it seems, may not be in them. The deficit may well be in us.

If those numbers count, we do not have a vocation crisis in the Church at all. We have, however, a crisis of significance and a crisis of spirituality. But the search for significance and spirituality go far deeper than change and far deeper than conformity; they demand renewal rather than adaptation. And they demand unity of vision and breadth of vision, unity of community and variety of community, unity of members and diversity of members at the same time.

The problem is whether or not such a thing can be done. When is too much conformity, on the one hand, and too much open-endedness on the other, inimical to the task of building community today?

Every community, canonical or not, must be built around a center. In the past, for religious communities, the center has been gender or ethnicity or ministry. There were women's communities and men's communities; German communities and Italian communities; teaching communities and nursing communities. Selectivity was woven right into the nature of the community itself. The "None-other-need-apply" message was loud and clear. For those outlanders who did, assimilation and homogenization was the foregone conclusion. In these groups, how a thing was done quickly became a great deal more important than what was done. And, for all their talk of immersion in the world and identity with the poor, the distance grew between themselves and the rest of the Church until, in a rarified way, they soon began to emerge from their spiritual cocoons every day, only to practice their trade at regular intervals and then, at the end of the work, to disappear into them quietly and unnoticed and together again at night.

After over 20 years of experimentation and outreach, many religious communities are now almost at the other extreme. In this period, it is often hard to tell what the community, as community, does and even, sometimes, what the community, as community, is. One at a time they live their poured-out lives in the midst of a busy world, good professionals and good people, but largely without context or identity.

In these circumstances, the questions of renewal, unity, selectivity and formation become one.

The old model says control is the answer. But where conformity is the criteria, only those can come who are willing to become what everyone else is. The new model sees commitment as sufficient. But if a sense of personal commitment is the only requirement, anyone can come who calls themselves called. I would argue that if significance and spirituality are the hallmarks of religious life, then the answer to selection lies somewhere in between these two extremes of sheer discipline and vague interest.

The key, I think, lies in the identity—not of the individual members—but of the community itself.

It can be very difficult now to know what religious communities are all about. Even the most controlled, most conservative, most concentrated groups lack a compelling identity. Why enter to teach? Anyone can teach, and even in Catholic schools. Why enter to do parish work? More and more laity are doing parish work everyday. And why enter for asceticism? Negative discipline or asceticisms no longer, on the whole, either enamor or assure. Modern psychology and creation theology have both cast doubt on the value of penance for its own sake.

Post-renewal communities, on the other hand, show differences in extreme. What they often fail to do is communicate a clear reason for being together at all. If the members do not live together or work together or pray together, what compelling purpose brings them together and how is it to be recognized, either by those inside the community or by those outside it? And who would know what it was when they saw them, even if they did live together and work together and pray together?

Whatever the form, however, groups that demand a single profile of spiritual fulfillment and groups that require no identity at all each limit themselves to a considerable kind of sameness: those that are all together exactly what someone wants them to be and those who share only enough past things in common—denomination, associations, training, language, ethnic identity—to be able to need little else to know who they are.

To be witness communities these days, however, I submit that selectivity in community must now become more a matter of vision than of ministry or good will. It is the vision that must both identify and determine the members, not works—though the works are good—and not personal preference and past historical profiles—though community life is indeed a good and personally enriching way to live that has grown many of us up in a culture that no longer exists.

The fact is that people join groups, not simply because the groups are like them, but because groups enable us to do together what we could not possibly do alone. Groups, in other words, become the vehicle of our aspirations. We do not join groups to be what the group wants to be or to do what the group wants to do.

We join groups to become what we know we must become and to do what we know we must do and because, finally, for us, we see this group as the most effective way to be whatever that is.

The history of traditional religious life, then, demonstrates clearly that a group who doesn't know what it is about in this day and age will do one of two things: Either it will force people to become something for its own sake or it will enable people to become little more than they would be without it. The question of membership and selectivity clearly becomes a question of group identity and purpose itself. The secret is not in doing different things but in doing things differently. The function of religious life in this era is certainly, more than ever, to be leaven rather than labor force, sign rather than subculture.

But if religious life is to be a sign of the coming Kingdom of God, then membership can hardly be focused on single categories of people. And if the vision that propels religious life is global, it can hardly be parochial in its membership.

As a result of these realities, two concepts are emerging quickly among religious communities everywhere and among the newer forms of intentional communities as well. The first is the concept of the Corporate Commitment. The second is the diversification of membership among committed and non-committed, young and old, men and women, Catholic and non-Catholic. The question in the 20th century becomes "What can possibly be called the global village?"

The Corporate Commitment: Its Relation to Formation and Membership

If the secret to a religious vocation is significance and spirituality, then we have to ask ourselves whether the problem of declining vocations might not lie in the fact that somehow we are failing to demonstrate that, as groups, we are really about the important things of our time in important ways.

We are seen too often, it seems, as doing either too little or too much. It is too little to have only schools when Africa is starving and the West is stuffing itself with nuclear bombs above the heavens and below the sea. It is too much to have religious in every kind of institution in the country, but have no clear reason for them to be there, while the poor get poorer and the strong get stronger. Institutions, in other words, seem to weigh us down and individual ministries seem to fade us out of the center of things, the core of things, the heart of things, the sin of things. In one instance, a lot of teachers call themselves religious, and so people who are willing to teach become the membership. In the other situation, a lot of apparently independent professionals call themselves religious, and so people who are willing to live a vowed life alone work with all their might in their corner of the world to live life well and to make it better for others. The message to new groups is clear: a task too tightly defined can cut the community off from the world it says it wants to serve; a task too loosely-defined can cast a group adrift without purpose and without meaning.

There is another alternative, however. Communities with a Corporate Commitment, rather than a commitment to institutional works or no clear commitment to any particular work at all, form their members in its theology and its goals and then send them into all their personal arenas to spread the net of the commitment and leaven the system at every level, in every area, as a community.

A Corporate Commitment, in other words, is a community resolve to promote, effect or support a major idea or concept or beatitude or Biblical truth that is compatible with the community charism and essential to the upbringing of the Kingdom in our time, by participating in actions as a community and by investment of the individual members in bringing that idea to consciousness in whatever personal ministries they may undertake. A Franciscan community, then, might choose to concentrate on issues of hunger; a Benedictine group on issues of international peace; a Dominican congregation on issues of economic education; a missionary community on Soviet-American relations, a peace community on the creation of an environment open to international agreement, a charismatic community on the renewal of liturgical life.

In each instance, the community as community would take upon itself the distribution of community monies to promote the enterprise, or the presentation of community programs to conscienticize others, or the publication of educational materials for the Church at large. Then, every individual member of the community would determine how to bring the Corporate Commitment to her own life works and milieu. Older members might form prayer groups or talk to their families about the question. Younger or more active religious would bring the issue into their own hospital work, or classrooms, or parishes, or program themes. Here diversity is of the essence of witness. Here differences become the strength. Here significance and spirituality are yoked. Here people see a community at work, promoting, tithing, supporting, enabling, educating, energizing. Here you find a peacemaking community, or a liberation community, or a social justice community, not a religious organization with a few peaceniks or feminists or social activists in it. Here every situation is a situation for ministry and every additional person strengthens the community outreach. What the community stands for, they stand for as an entire witnessing group. And people can see it. And people know it because the same message is coming from everywhere, both individually and as a group.

In this situation, formation depends on bringing the Gospel to the here and now, to steeping the members in the theological, spiritual, communal, liturgical, ascetical and professional implications of the issue. And membership selection becomes a matter, then, of determining only who is intent on bringing the Gospel to the human condition rather than of bringing a person to a specific task.

Significance is guarded by a regular review of the Corporate Commitment for relevance and urgency and human need. Spirituality is geared to developing in the members the qualities necessary to weld both the community and the members together, by enabling them to grow in the virtues and insights needed to become a community of peace or equality or compassion or justice.

Leaven and witness and breadth of association and breadth of response begin quickly to mark the community with a Corporate Commitment. Neither control nor individual good works become enough to describe the character of this kind of a community. The Corporate Commitment makes it necessary for the group to work together, to be something together, to stand for something together. Imagine the impact on the world if 100,000 religious decided on any given day of the week to go to jail together to end the nuclear arms race as they once decided to go to schools together to end illiteracy.

The Relationship Between Selectivity and Membership

But communities with a clear community ministry who are clearly open to the world and open to its multiple peoples will become significant to all sorts of people: to the poor, to the disenfranchised, to the powerless, to the oppressed, to the charismatic, to the prophetic, to the young, to the old, to men and to women, to the married and to the single. And then the question becomes, how can all of these differences be reconciled? Is this really one community or is it no community at all? Is such a conglomeration of people really impossible? And if so, how?

In the first place, a community with a new focus on meaning and ministry suddenly discovers that all the categories that once hemmed it in or hemmed it out no longer hold. The sacred and the secular are forever joined. Like Jeremiah calling the people to live their political lives in the spirit of the God who called them to be a people, the community that finds itself with the task of enabling creation to go on creating in our day can hardly call any way that is doable unclean or anyone who wants to do it unacceptable. The person who answers the phone in the housing co-op is as much ministering as the person who leaflets the Federal Housing Office. The member who works in what is apparently a totally-unrelated position to get enough money to enable the community to have some of its members working for no pay at all with the homeless in the city parks is as involved and as significant as the members who manage the community low-rent housing project. Employed and unemployed, the active and the retired, the agents of the institution and the separately-employed members, the prayer leaders and the social activists, then, are all part of the same great ministry, all carriers of the same great work, all builders of the same Gospel world, all holders of the same social impact.

No wonder, then, that people once not called "religious" begin to gravitate toward the community and draw their energy from it and look to it for leadership. No aliens here, the entire Christian community finds something of meaning, and membership begins to take several forms: those for whom the core community will be their entire life, their sole identity, the totality of their focus; those for whom the community becomes a spiritual and apostolic guide; and those for whom the community becomes a sign of hope of the unity of all, whether they themselves share the same tradition or not.

Professed members, core members, associates, oblates, co-disciples or whatever the terms used to designate different forms of community identity, these people all drink from the same spring and carry the freshness of it together. People begin to enter the community at all ages, from all walks of life, with no specific work but only the creation of an alternate world and a spiritual way of life in mind. And the community begins to see them, not as people to be re-formed but people to be integrated into the vision of the whole.

In monastic communities, the sharing of life and prayer and ministry together becomes the staple of their witness. In apostolic congregations, the conduct of the mission out of a common Gospel perspective becomes the order of the whole. In intentional communities, too, the life-style and work must become secondary to the group intention to be a Gospel group, or when cultural change comes, change kills. But whatever form the group takes, there is no doubt that here is a group made up of several groups perhaps but all gathered together around the Gospel alone for the sake of the world. There are no aliens here, either within the core community or outside of it. This kind of religious life is about world-building and the vantage point of the Gospel.

Communities such as these know, as did the disciples on Mount Tabor, that the function of community life is spiritual transfiguration, but that community life is not a place for building booths. It is only the starting point from which they must travel with the newly-magnetic Christ to the crowded, dirty, needy towns below.

9
An Open Letter to the U.S. Bishops

Dear Bishops,

One of my most hopeful moments of Church came when the bishops of the United States were willing to wrestle with the questions of nuclear morality in a nuclear world. One of my most disappointing moments, on the other hand, came when you failed to say that deterrence that is aimed at the destruction of the globe is morally unacceptable, that a defense system that has already begun to erode the social fiber of our country with its lustful, gluttonous, profligate use of resources, which could and should be better used to assure human development rather than to plot human destruction, could possibly be a sinless activity.

How can we possibly say that what is immoral to use is moral to design and develop and deploy?

How can we possibly say that to abort a fetus is morally wrong but that the weapons intended only to abort the entire human race is not?

How can we possibly make ourselves and our generation more worthy of the ultimate act of retaliation than any other possible moment in history?

Isn't the arrogance of those postures alone a sin against the Holy Spirit?

How is it that we can ask people to be prepared to die in nuclear warfare in the name of a "defense" that is destructive, but refuse to ask them to be prepared to die in passive resistance in the name of the Gospel? All that would happen to us if we faced a nuclear attack without weapons is that we would die, but isn't that the very posture that we clearly espouse even now in the name of "defense"?

And isn't that precisely the kind of deterrence that we expect from the non-nuclear world even now?

The point is that we say that nuclear weapons alone can be a deterrence to nuclear war. But surely there is a rational and Christian deterrence as well that would be equally effective. All that would happen to us if we faced a nuclear attack, with nuclear weapons, is that we would die. All that would happen to us if we faced a nuclear attack, without our nuclear weapons, is that we would die. And in each case, the enemy would simply destroy what they wanted and threaten their own existence as well. The posture that we now espouse in the name of "defense," then, makes us no less vulnerable, but it takes from the poor while we practice it and it holds the world hostage to fear while we stockpile more and always more demonic danger. The difference is that in refusing ourselves to threaten a nuclear retaliation, or worse, "pre-emptive strike," we would not have set out to destroy creation in the doing.

An even greater question, perhaps, for us as Church may be: why is it that the unilateral initiatives for weapons destruction must come from an atheist General Secretary of a Communist State rather than from the Roman Catholic Bishops of a professedly Christian nation?

The fact is that governments and political systems, economic theories and institutional philosophies, kings and presidents, emperors and premiers, all come and go, come and go. Is this system, culture, era, epoch, or political arena of ours really worth the price: the loss of human services and education and housing and health now, the loss of all our futures as well as the cost of all glories of our past, the possible loss of the planet itself? Would any other era think so? Is any form of self-defense, then, acceptable, regardless of its consequences and its costs? Is becoming what we hate the Christian answer to the fears of this world? Is this the message of the Gospel for which we stand?

It was a Christian state that designed the Holocaust and Christian countries that waged the Inquisition and Christian states that burned witches and napalmed Vietnamese villages and used the atomic bomb, not once but twice, for experimental purposes. Now with all the planet and universal human morality and civilization itself at stake, in an age when errors cannot be forgiven, we are begging you, lead this Christian state to more than that.

I am asking you to reject the balance-of-terror game in favor of turning this country to Truth and Light as you have in so many other issues: the labor movement and religious freedom and human rights.

The Rule of Benedict requires humility as the cornerstone of a spirituality built in the patriarchal culture of imperial Rome. We need that same humility now from the Church. Call this country to negotiations, to human respect, to faith and to humility in our dealing with both the little and the great ones of this world. As long as the bishops of the country give credence to a militarism based on arrogance and fear and paranoia and power and pride, it will be called moral even though it isn't.

There is an ancient proverb that teaches, "Wherever there is excess in anything, something is lacking." Finish the fine work you have begun and give this nation what it lacks, to its peril, in its excessive militarism, the challenge of peace.

10

Religion and Peace

There are two insights that may best define the role of religion in peace-making at this moment in history. The first comes from Nazim Hikmet who wrote in 1950:

"This life is not a joke.
You must take it seriously.
Seriously enough to find yourself
Up against a wall, maybe, with your wrists bound."

The second comes from Bishop Desmond Tutu who teaches, "If you are neutral in situations of injustice, you have chosen the side of the oppressor. If an elephant has his foot on the tail of the mouse and you say that you are neutral, the mouse will not appreciate your neutrality."

The call is clear. If we want a nuclear free world in the 90's, we are going to have to take the present seriously enough not to be neutral about the immoral.

The stakes are high; the whole world is at risk; the agenda is deceptive; what looks like defense is really total destruction and the consequences are unforgiving.

But this is not the first time in history that calamity has been an option. The only difference between now and past times is that in our time it is the entire planet, not simply one single people that is at stake. In times before this one, if Germany destroyed Poland, only Poland would be lost. One false move, one bad judgment, one act of mad terrorism, one technical mistake, one chauvinistic theological heresy, one more elected Hitler and it is our entire world that will be extinguished. Today, in this age, Chernobyl is not a local problem. Today, not just soldiers and ships and military installations will be the targets and the cost of war. No, in the next war, in nuclear war, it will be child care centers and homes for the elderly and ice cream stores and the Hermitage and the Metropolitan Museum of Art and small neighborhood restaurants that will go, and they all will go. No prisoners taken. No bounty reaped. No ransoms paid in this war without winners that we are both prepared to wage. Clearly, religion today must rise above a theology of tribal gods to a theology of creation, to a theology of universal love and cosmic unity, or religion will simply become another kind of pawn on the playing field of the military.

So, the question is: Is there anything we can learn from the religion of another age to save us from ourselves in this one? Well, we do get a clue, I think, from the Scriptures of the Old Testament. The interesting thing is that Israel, too, faced destruction after destruction. And in each case, prophets came to warn the people. The fascinating truth is, however, that none of the prophets ever came to tell the Israelites how to fight the war or how to win the war or, even, how to survive the war. No, the prophets simply spoke the will of God to remind Israel of the reasons for the wars. The prophets came to recall to their senses a people who had stopped making connections. And the prophets, all of them, always said the same thing: "Calamity is coming upon us because . . . you have been unjust to the widows, you have forgotten the orphans, you have oppressed the outcast, you have persecuted the foreigners. And you have worshipped false gods." Finally, the prophets always spoke to their own. They never spoke to the enemy. They said to their own country: "You have gone astray from the God of Gods. You have set your hearts on the wrong things. You have lost your soul to profit or prejudice or power." Religion that supports the pursuit of national idolatry, in other words, is no religion at all. It may be tribalism. It may be magic. It may be civic cheerleading, but it is not religion. It is not the spirit that seeks to bind all things together in the love of the one God.

The function of religion is to tell us when we're lost. When we've gone sour, when we've gone sick. When we're not making connections anymore. The prophets Amos and Jeremiah and Isaiah all warned against the kind of national blindness that turned dark into light, and differences into distinctions, and evil into good, and down into up. Amos and Jeremiah and Isaiah insisted on unmasking the irrational in all of Israel's rationalizations: That religious services were an acceptable substitute for religious integrity; that it is possible to compromise conscience in the name of citizenship; that business is better than compassion.

And, today, too, it seems, religion as call to cosmic consciousness must unmask our feeble rationalization that the purpose of nuclear deterrence is peace. When we have 99% more nuclear weapons than are necessary to ward off a nuclear war and which threaten this entire planet with nuclear devastation, no real religion can abide it. Religion today must unmask the rationalizations it takes to keep the United States and the Soviet Union in the business of making weapons while the poor the world over struggle to eat, and the illiterate struggle to get educated, and families struggle to raise children, and the homeless struggle for decent shelter, and workers struggle for their dignity and their dreams. We are using our best resources and the best research minds we have in the best universities in our countries on weapons of universal destruction rather than on technology for universal development. Surely religion cannot suffer this kind of sin in the name of patriotism. Surely religion must unmask and refuse the enemy-bashing that it takes to make a people willing to commit national suicide.

The problem is that in a world where every decent thing that humankind has ever done is now in peril, both our future and our past, both Shakespeare and the space shuttle, we may no longer have the luxury of allowing our governments to choose our enemies for us. We may have no choice but the Gospel. We badly need a religion that reminds us always that we are all one, that sin in the name of national security is still sin, that wisdom lies in awareness, that peace lies in miracles of mind of our own making and that prophecy lies in helping a people to make connections. We need a religion that reminds us that it isn't just nuclearism itself that we must question in the 90s. It is, as well, the attitudes that make nuclearism possible. We have to remind the modern world, with the prophets that any nation that forgets the other, the widowed and the orphaned, the outcast and the foreigners, the oneness of creation and all its peoples, is asking for war, is already at war, is losing the war.

In tests of geographic literacy conducted in the West within the last six months, people could not identify the largest cities on the globe despite the fact that these are the most volatile, fastest-growing, neediest sections of the world, where poverty and power and profit and problems designed to ignite the world are already at play. If religion is to be religion, we must begin to call people, in the name of the Gospel, to make the connections among poverty, oppression and peace. Theologies of Armageddon and Crusader mentalities and just war theories and civil religion must all give way now to universal unity and nuclear pacifism and cries for justice, internal as well as external, local as well as global, because those are the cornerstones of peace.

The point is that, often in the name of religion, we have made ourselves the center of the universe. We have failed to make the connections. If we are truly religious people, we must learn to understand differences. We must learn to respect differing needs. We must learn that nuclear superiority may be precisely what is making us morally inferior in everything else. We have to learn to make connections. Our widows who must work to live, our children whose schools are poor, our outcasts whose lives are limited, our foreigners who look to us for help stand in mute conviction of two countries that have, for all practical purposes, been at war within themselves for 20 years and whose weapons are destroying their own.

Or let's put it this way. Analysts tell us that if we had simply chosen to produce two less nuclear-powered aircraft in 1986, we could have restored the entire CETA program whose retraining system could have forstalled the massive industrial displacement of this country. The production of one fewer Trident submarines could have restored all the food stamp cuts in the United States. If, as a nation, we had built one less Cruise missle, we would have been able to maintain all the subsidized housing programs for the poor, the handicapped, and the elderly that the Reagan administration so ruthlessly eliminated.

In this country, the factory system has become obsolete; people are out of work with no hope of learning new skills; hardworking people fear the economic hardship of old age in the richest country in the world because we want weapons we say we'll never use.

And that's a sin. That's a subject that religion must speak to. Why? Because it isn't enough simply to count the missiles that we have and they have. We have to begin to ask why we have them and what people can't have as long as we continue to gorge ourselves with weapons we clearly don't need and which probably won't work. This is, after all, peacetime, isn't it? Or has wartime become our way of life?

We have to stop believing that "deterrence" works, is moral. Deterrence has already begun to destroy our nations. It is choking our farms, and eroding our educational system, and limiting our cities, and depressing our national growth. National deterioration is nuclearism turned upon ourselves. It is destructive of people, our own people, and so it is immoral. We have to come to see that individualism that absolves us from responsibility is nuclearism turned upon ourselves. Even if I only weld the rivets on nuclear missiles, I am responsible for them. Even if I only do the scientific calculations that make the missiles possible, I am responsible for them. Real religion, authentic religion, teaches us to make the connections.

Our debt is not to past world tensions; our debt is to future world growth. There is simply no difference now between global war and global suicide. And that is sin. Try to imagine anyone supporting the notion that the entire world should have been destroyed by nuclear war in order to defend Socrates' Greece or Napoleon's France or Kaiser Wilhelm's Germany. But if none of those great moments in history would have merited the distinction of nuclear destruction, then why this one? How are we the last great moment of human development, after which nothing else is worth striving toward?

We need more conscience than this. We need real religion, not religious justification for the morally unjustifiable. No, the truth is that nuclear weapons are not a political question. Nuclear weapons are, first and foremost, a moral and a theological question. To threaten all love, all wisdom, and all creativity at one time is immoral under any provocation. And religion, to be authentic, must speak to that. Religion is not a private exercise of the pious. Religion cannot be the tool of the state. Religion must not be simply the social sign of the believing but ineffective. Religion must open the soul to things beyond us, and cost the heart for the other, and spend the body for the creation of a better world. To say that we allow religion but separate church and state, when what we really mean is that religion must be domesticated, that no one must ever call the conscience of the king, is no religion at all. Devotion is not religion. Devotion comforts and soothes the individual. Religion confronts and challenges the individual. The function of religion, in other words, the function of the prophet, is to speak truth to power.

Religion must not be allowed to subsume the state, true. History is full of instances where religion was the problem. But the state must not be allowed to smother the voice of religion or the cry of human conscience will be lost to the world. To say we permit religion but stifle its voice on political issues is like saying that we permit education but forbid schools. And good will is not enough. Ethics only describes right action, but religion shapes right hearts. Action without vision is not enough. Ethics is devoted to the highest of human goods. Religion is committed to the fullness of divine possibility. Ethics tells us who we are. Religion tells us who we can be. We need religion to enable us to transcend ourselves for others and to live for something greater than ourselves; to speak the word of God to a world that has made itself its highest good.

Once upon a time, the elder asked the disciples which was more important, wisdom or action. The disciples were unanimous. "Action, of course," they said. "Of what use is wisdom that does not show itself in action?" And the elder said, "And of what use is action that proceeds from an unenlightened heart?"

We have action aplenty in our times, some of it wonderful, some of it deadly. How does such talent lead to such destructiveness if not because it is unbridled, undirected and blind.

A commitment to creation, a call to national conscience, and a sense of human connectedness is the vision that religion must bring to the peacemaking agenda for the 90s. We must be a voice for the voiceless; we must be a clear call to cosmic conscience; we must turn the world around, one heart at a time. That's the awareness we need now; those are the miracles waiting to be worked by me and you; that is what is needed to raise piety to the status of religion; that is the only thing that will save us from ourselves.

11
Peacemaking and Prophetic Vision

There are two stories that may best define prophetic vision and the peacemaking agenda of the 90s:

The first story comes from ancient Sufi tradition. Once upon a time, the story goes, a disciple came riding on his camel to the tent of his Sufi Master. He dismounted and walked right into the tent, bowed low and said, "So great is my trust in God that I have left my camel outside untied, convinced that God protects the interests of those who love him."

But the Master said, "Go tie your camel, you fool! God cannot be bothered doing for you what you are perfectly capable of doing for yourself."

The second story comes from the writings of the Hasidim: This tale relates that, once upon a time, an old rabbi became blind. He could neither read nor write nor look at the faces of those who came to visit him.

Then one day, a faith healer said to him, "Entrust yourself to my care and I will heal your blindness."

But the Rabbi said to him, "There will be no need for that. The fact is that I am already able to see everything that I need to."

The wisdom of the ancients is as clear and as valid as ever: If we want a nuclear-free world in the 90s, we are going to have to concentrate on developing insight and on doing for ourselves what that insight demands. The stakes are high; the agenda is deceptive; and the consequences are unforgiving. For the first time in the history of the human race, we are capable of destroying it. For the first time in the history of the human race, we are determined to do so.

The very idea is overwhelming. And yet this is not the first time in history that calamity has been an option. The only difference between now and past times is that in our time it is the entire planet, not simply one single people, that is at stake. In times before this one, if Germany destroyed Poland, it was only Poland that was exterminated. If Japan conquered China, it was only the Chinese who would disappear. If Britain consumed India, it was only India that would be lost. But now, one false move, one bad judgment, one act of mad terrorism, one technical mistake, one more elected Hitler, and it is our entire world that will be extinguished.

Today, in this age, Chernobyl is not a local problem. Today, Three Mile Island is not a local technical fluke. The downwind route of nuclear waste has long ago erased the national borders that once made us secure. What is worse, today not just soldiers and ships and military installations will be the targets and the cost of war. No, in the next war, in nuclear war, it will be child care centers and homes for the elderly and ice cream stores and the French Quarter and the Metropolitan Museum of Art and small neighborhood restaurants and Disney World that will go, in their country and in our country and everywhere. No prisoners taken. No bounty reaped. No ransoms paid in the war without winners that we have set out to wage.

So, the question is: Isn't there anything we can learn from another age to save us from ourselves in this one? Isn't there anything we can do to avoid destruction at our own hands?

Well, we get a clue, I think, from the Hebrew Scriptures. There calamity was as common as the social circus that always preceded it.

The interesting thing is that Israel faced destruction after destruction and, in each case, prophets came to warn the people. The fascinating truth, however, is that none of the prophets ever came to tell the Israelites how to fight the war or how to win the war or even how to survive the war. No, the Jewish prophets were simply sent by God to remind Israel of the reasons for the wars. The prophets came to recall to their senses a people who had stopped making connections. And the prophets, all of them, always said the same thing: This calamity is coming upon this nation because . . . you have been unjust to the widows, you have forgotten the orphans, you have oppressed the outcast and you have persecuted the foreigners. You have gone astray after baubles and bangles. You have put your hearts on the wrong things. You have lost your soul to power and profit and prejudice. You've gone soft. You've gone sour. You've gone sick. Your insight is dull and and your will to good is numbed. You don't make connections anymore.

I would argue that when a people, any people, cease to make connections, they become prey to their own need for force. When a country stops making social connections, then it has to use force to keep the foreigners in line. And they have to use force to keep its allies in line. And pretty soon that nation will have to use force to keep its own people in line.

Amos and Jeremiah and Isaiah all warned against the kind of national blindness that turned dark into light, and evil into good and down into up. Amos and Jeremiah and Isaiah insisted on unmasking the irrational in all of Israel's rationalizations:

Isaiah unmasked the rationalization that religious exercises were a graced substitute for integrity, or as virtuous as virtue or as good as justice to the neighbor.

Jeremiah unmasked the rationalization that Israel could consort with compromise and compromise with conscience and thrive.

Amos unmasked the rationalization that business could possibly demand "selling the poor man for a pair of shoes."

And today Amos and Jeremiah and Isaiah would not stand for the feeble rationalization that the purpose of nuclear deterrence is peace when we have 99% more nuclear weapons than we need to ward off a nuclear war, and when only two such weapons could plunge this entire planet into nuclear devastation.

Amos and Jeremiah and Isaiah would not have tolerated the rationalizations it takes to keep the United States in the business of making weapons while the poor the world over struggle to eat, and the illiterate struggle to get educated, and families struggle to raise children and the homeless struggle for shelter and workers struggle for their dignity and their dreams. We use our best resources and the best research minds we have in the best universities in this country to make bombs; to inflate the largest military budget we've ever had; to build Star Wars, the scientific fiction that will do nothing but soak up our resources and scorch our souls.

Amos and Jeremiah and Isaiah would not have tolerated the enemy-bashing that it takes to make a people willing to commit national suicide for the sake of the military-industrial complex.

We have confused loving the country with being willing to die for the government, and we call that patriotism. But there is a patriotism that demands the best from us as well as the worst. There is a kind of patriotism that demanded the end to slavery and withdrawal from Vietnam and the right to conscientious objection and the release of the Pentagon Papers and the testimony of a John Dean. And that is the kind of patriotism that is surely needed now in an era when our technology matches our consumerism, our greed and our paranoia. It is that kind of patriotism that matches the goodness of the people and the real character of the land. It is that kind of patriotism that the prophets were asking for when they asked for fidelity to a covenant that rested on righteousness and responsibility.

Amos and Jeremiah and Isaiah would ask why it is, if Communism is the problem, if Communism is the paralyzing fear that keeps us producing more for destruction than for development in this country, in the richest country of the world, then why isn't Communist China our enemy anymore; and if it's freedom of religion we're preserving, why isn't Mexico with its constitutional provisions against the practice of religion our enemy; and why aren't Poland and Hungary and the Communist members of the parliament of Italy our enemy? Why don't we ascribe to them the same motives and menace that we project onto the Soviet Union? And if human rights is the issue, why is the apartheid policy of South Africa and the *disapericido* policy of El Salvador and the refugee problem of the Middle East less of a diplomatic problem for us than the emigration policies of the Soviet Union? The point is not whether or not the Soviet Union is right or wrong; the point is that there must be reasons under our reasons or the Soviet Union wouldn't be and couldn't be our only problem.

Isn't it possible that the real problem is that Mexico and Poland and Italy and China don't threaten our markets or our superior status in the world like the Soviet Union does? Isn't it possible, in other words, that if we didn't have the Soviet Union to call the enemy, we would have to invent her in order to go on justifying the fact that more than 40 years after the end of World War II we still have not converted to peacetime industry, where money is made on toasters instead of on plutonium trigger-fingers for nuclear bombs?

Don't we really need an enemy to explain why 35,000 businesses receive military contracts and 150,000 others do subcontracting in weapons and weapons alone in a country not at war?

Don't we really need an enemy to explain why we go on day after day after day producing what we say we'll never use, and failing to supply what we need but say we can't afford to produce: like quality education and universal daycare and catastrophic medical insurance and housing instead of tent cities for the poor of the richest country in the world. Indeed, wisdom lies in insight. And peace lies in matching our character to our sense of meaning. And prophecy lies in making connections.

It isn't just nuclearism itself, though, that we must question in the 90s: It is the attitudes that make nuclearism possible and the sighted blind and the otherwise compassionate hard-hearted that you and I must begin to address. We have to begin to make connections. We have to start seeing the unseeable and questioning the unquestionable. We have to remind the United States with the prophets that any nation that forgets the widowed and the orphaned and the outcast and the foreigners is asking for war, is already at war, is losing the war. If the leadership of the Western world is in the hands of the United States of America, there is something we had better all soon realize before we trust ourselves more than the temper of this land deserves. A short test may illustrate the present situation best:

1. Which of the following five cities is the largest? What is its population? New York/ Tokyo/ Beijing/ Mexico City/ Calcutta.

2. What is the current population of the United States?

3. In what country are the Sandinistas and Contras fighting? Iran, Lebanon, Nicaragua or Afghanistan.

4. Name five members of the NATO countries.

5. Name five members of the Warsaw Pact.

6. In what country is apartheid an official policy?

7. What is the capital of the United States?

8. Name 15 countries of Africa.

9. On an unmarked world map in your head, locate Central America, the Pacific Ocean and the Persian Gulf.

On this international survey, which was conducted in eight countries by the Gallup organization, Americans ranked sixth, ahead only of Italy and Mexico. But of young U.S. adults, adults between the ages of 18 and 24, adults who will lead this country or at least vote for its leaders, Americans who expect to lead the entire Western world, those U.S. respondents scored dead last, below every other country surveyed.

The fact is that, though only 15% of the Americans surveyed knew it, the largest, poorest city of the world is Mexico City, 20 million strong, and it sits on our borders getting bigger and poorer every year, looking for food and wages. But instead of helping them to strengthen themselves in order to strengthen us, we put money into bombs.

The fact is that 57% of the Americans asked did not know that the current population of the United States is almost 300 million. Yet, since the 1970s, over half of our workers, according to Newman's newly-released anthropological study of downward mobility in the United States, professionals as well as blue-collar workers, managers as well as laborers, high-income earners as well as low-income farmers, have found themselves unemployed or their incomes cut, not because they failed to produce but because the work they were in has simply ceased to exist. Though the population continues to rise, in other words, we go on putting more money into bullets that don't create jobs unless they're used, of course, rather than into job retraining programs or industrial development that could. We must begin to make the connections. We must begin to make the connections.

The fact is that though 50% of the survey population thought otherwise, the Sandinistas and the Contras are not fighting in the Middle East or on the borders of the Soviet Union. They are fighting on the fringe of our own territory on this continent and a mistake of diplomacy there, a show of force there, may well affect the future of this nation itself, for decades to come. Yet, at the same time, we just put secret U. S. money into that undeclared war in defiance of our own national laws, but we put no new money whatsoever into national daycare programs to care for the children that are our own future.

The ten members of NATO and the five members of the Warsaw Pact are countries we are supposed to fight for or fight with at any given moment, but two thirds of the Americans tested had no idea who they are or, apparently, what they need and what they want if we do go to war with them. That means, too, that they can't read a newspaper and get any clear idea of the implications of what a NATO story really means to them.

Five percent of the U.S. citizens tested did not know that Washington, D.C. is the capital of this country.

Only 10% of the Americans could name 15 countries in the fastest-growing continent in the world, Africa, though Africa is the rising giant of the world.

Seventy-five percent of us could not locate the Persian Gulf, though we are risking life and limb and a third World War there.

Forty-five percent of us did not know where Central America is located. Twenty percent of the Americans tested could not name a single country in Europe and almost 50% of us could not find England or France or Spain on a map.

We have made ourselves the center of the universe but we are failing to make the connections. We are peddling insular thinking in a world where national borders have already disappeared in finances and industry and trade and ecological reality. And we say that we are the ones who are going to lead this world? In 1992 all the boundaries of the European Economic Market are scheduled to fall, and if and when that happens, that single new commercial entity will control more money, touch more markets and serve more consumers than all of U.S. trade and industry put together.

Konrad Adenauer said once: "We all live under the same sky, but we don't all have the same horizons." The implications are clear. We have to learn to understand differences or we will never learn to respect differing needs. We have to learn that nuclear superiority may be precisely what is making us inferior in everything else. We have to learn to make connections.

We have to stop believing that "deterrence," the policy of indiscriminate extermination of the innocent, the policy that says that two thirds of every disposable tax dollar collected can go to destruction rather than to development, we have to stop believing that a policy like that works, is effective, is moral. Deterrence has already begun to destroy this nation. Deterrence has already begun to defeat this nation. Deterrence has already begun to reduce this nation to rubble. It has leveled our farms and robbed our elderly and eroded our educational system and eliminated our industries.

We have to come to see that geographic illiteracy and educational deterioration is nuclearism turned upon ourselves.

We have to come to see that an individualism that absolves us from responsibility in a society where responsibility has become a fiction is nuclearism turned upon ourselves. We have to come to see that the assembly line mentality of this world has really become an assembly line morality as well: Because I only weld the rivets on cruise missiles, I'm not responsible for them. Because I only do the scientific calculations that make the missiles possible, I'm not responsible for them. Because I only vote for the people who are wedded to them, I'm not responsible for them. We have to begin to make the connections.

We have to begin to see ourselves as citizens of the world as well as of the country, because, like it or not, we are Siamese-twinned to every other people of the world. Whatever hurts them will eventually, these days, come to hurt us, too. Whatever corrodes the United States will soon lower the living standard of the entire world. Our debt is not to past world tensions; our debt is to future world growth. We cannot live in the 50s forever. There is simply no difference now between global war and global suicide. Try to imagine anyone supporting the notion that the entire world should have been destroyed by nuclear war in order to defend Socrates' Greece, or the Holy Roman Empire, or Napoleon's France, or Peter the Great's Russia, or Jefferson Davis' Confederate States or Kaiser Wilhelm's Germany or Peter Botha's South Africa.

But if none of those great moments in history would have merited the distinction of nuclear destruction, then why this one? If none of those days, in the long light of history, deserve the ultimate act of self-destruction, why this one of ours? In exactly what ways are this culture and these countries worthy of the annihilation of the world? How are we the last great moment of human development, after which nothing else is worth striving toward? Or, on the other hand, in what way is this world of ours so decadent, so decrepit, so totally morally destitute that it does not deserve saving so that it can become something better? How is it that you and your family are so evil or so useless that anyone ought to mark you as disposable enough to be the last of your kind? No, we are global citizens now. What one nation does affects all the others for all time and all its peoples.

We are one ecological system, one water system, one atmosphere, one great interlocking set of resources. The saber-rattling that comes with local political macho must give way now to human world interests. The days of adolescent gang wars on the international world scene must end and we must grow up with them.

Nuclear weapons are not a political question; the polis, the people, cannot possibly be improved by them. Nuclear weapons are not a defense question; we cannot possibly be "defended" by them. Nuclear weapons are first and foremost a moral and theological question. To threaten all love, all wisdom and all creativity at one time is illegitimate and immoral under any provocation. And we must not be complacent. We hold 95% more nuclear weapons than it would take to unleash the nuclear winter that would starve and freeze and radiate the entire globe after a nuclear exchange.

One INF treaty that is eliminating only 1% of the nuclear weapons we hold is not solving our problem, even though it is certainly changing the climate of our negotiations.

We must, finally, make a commitment to the haunting wisdom of a simple folk-tale: Once upon a time, in an isolated country, the story goes, some people noticed that the citizens who ate of a strange, new harvest in the land went stark, raving mad. So they went to the king to ask what they should do in such a dire situation.

And the wise old king said, "Well, since there is no other food available now, we are forced to eat of this food, but let us at least know that we are mad and let us send out messengers to the mountain top to warn the world against a similar sick harvest and insane act."

The fact is that we, you and I, must take nuclear arms seriously. It is one thing to accept an inadequate treaty with joy and hope, but it is not enough. We must work even harder now that we know that peace is possible. Human nature is weak. With nuclear weapons there is no way whatsoever to protect the globe from the sinful or the insane, both of whom have been as likely to be elected to power as to seize it. We must go to the top of the mountain, you and I, as messengers that a little nuclear disarmament is not enough; that the widows and the children and the outcasts and the foreigners are looking to us to give them their future; that insular thinking in a global world is madness; that we must learn to make connections.

The people of the United States have always seen themselves as having a unique mission and a unique spirit and a unique character. Well, we have never had a better opportunity to be unique than now, to show spirit than now, to develop character than now. What would be unique would be for us to continue our mission to the world with wisdom, not with weapons; with the promise of a better world, not with the threat of annihilation of this one.

The Scriptures remind us that once, with Israel in the middle of turmoil and in need of a savior, Samson arose. Samson was a Nazirite, a person who was specifically dedicated to goodness and justice, and he witnessed to his commitment to the will of God by giving up wine and not cutting his hair. Now the name Samson, or Shimson, meant "sunperson," and Samson epitomized the label: he was bright with life, alive with the light of goodness. But as Samson, the judge and savior, became more and more successful, he forgot the source of his power. He allowed himself to be tricked into cutting his hair, and he was captured. His eyes were put out and he was chained to a grinding stone where his glory was over and his good life was gone. Eventually, though, Samson's hair grew in again and his strength was restored. Then, on a feast day, with all his enemies gathered in one place, he stretched his strong and bulging arms around the pillars to which he had been attached for ridicule and, straining with all his might, he toppled the columns and brought the temple down on all his enemies.

And what do we learn from Samson? We clearly learn the tragic, fatal combination of power and blindness. Without the union of strength with vision, Samson destroyed himself with his enemies.

The story, I think, is a prophetic warning to the United States of America. Our brute strength cannot be impaired, that's true, but our vision can be lost. And there is nothing as destructive as the well-meant power of a blind, bewildered and frightened giant. The INF treaty is an attempt to chain a blind brute. It is a glass half-empty and a glass half-full. It is, indeed, a step to celebrate, a beginning to applaud, but it is not nearly the end of the road. The widows are waiting; the children are illiterate; the outcasts are poor; the foreigners are hungry.

We have the political strength to help to make a difference in this world. We have the moral responsibility to try. We have the obligation to follow the vision wherever it leads. How well the prophets understood when they said: Without vision, the people perish. Global literacy, wholism, connectedness, and a continuing commitment to go all the way to the end of this vital and life-giving road is the commitment we must bring to the peacemaking agenda for the 90s. May we in our time understand as well, speak as clearly, be as faithful, become as aware, work as many miracles, and bring as much prophetic vision in our risks for peace as those who have reached and risked for peace before us. That is the insight we need now. That is the task God has given to you and me to do. That is the only thing that will save us from ourselves. God knows we've had more than enough warning.

12

Haiti: Voices of Misery, Voices of Promise

6:30 pm Sunday

When the plane left Miami for Port-au-Prince I was tired, hot and a little apprehensive. I was anxious, too, at the thought of going to a country whose history is a series of private armies at war with one another and at odds with the people.

So why am I here? Bonhoeffer writes: "There is a meaning in every journey that is unknown to the traveler." I will have to let Haiti itself teach me why I'm here.

All the way down today I have read and reviewed material on the country: its history, its political situation, its poverty. But in the United States, we hardly even know where Haiti is—let alone what Haiti is. And worse, we don't care.

Only one thing I know for sure, then, as Pan Am #433 begins its descent. From the air, it is beautiful—an island coast, rugged hills, blue, blue water. The question is: What is its soul like? And why?

10:00 pm Sunday

The learnings have begun. Claudette Werleigh, the local organizer, and her husband Georges pick us up at the airport. The airport is a dirty, dingy place reminiscent of Cairo—only smaller. There were twelve of us and our luggage, packed into the Toyota van that clanged up one steep and winding road after another. People—all young—clogged the roads where no sidewalks ran, and the car lurched from one side to the other for miles. It was a tight, wet, jarring ride through a hot and humid night.

Foyer Solidarité, the place we are staying, is deceiving. It's a huge, plantation-style mansion at the top of a hill. At first I was almost shocked to see the marble and the wrought iron and the open veranda. But inside, everything was large and bare. It's clean. There are art posters proclaiming the Scriptures of the poor. There are wall frescoes in native style. But there's nothing else. No lovely furniture. No television. No hot water in the shower, the cold water a trickle. There were, however, beautiful flowers in each sparse bedroom.

We settled in together to eat a light supper of soup and salad and then to study the agenda. By eleven it finally got cool enough to sleep.

12:30 pm Monday

It has been quite a morning. First we went to the clinic run by the radical priest Aristide—if by radical you mean someone committed to the Church of the beatitudes. He has denounced the government and challenged the bishops to speak for the poor. As a result, he has enemies in multiple places. But not among the poor. When church officials removed him from his parish, St. Jean Bosco, the poor converged en masse on the cathedral till this tiny little order priest was reinstated.

To neutralize his power, they have taken away his parish and permit him to function only as a convent chaplain. After all, with no pulpit to preach from, what threat is he with the crowds?

Well, Jesus didn't have a synagogue to operate from either, and Merton didn't have a position, and Dorothy Day was not an institution woman. Aristide, if I can judge from what I saw this morning, is a figure to be reckoned with.

The clinic is a huge old house and courtyard on a side street of a lower middle class section of Port-au-Prince. Over 2,000 people have come to the clinic for medical help. In addition to that, he has a work program for street children, boys who have no money, no job, no education. He also teaches them to read. Some sleep there on old bare mattresses on a wet concrete floor when there is nowhere else to go.

Aristide himself is clearly revolutionary, a prophet, a scourge of the system. There have been several attempts on his life and, as we sat on the veranda overlooking the playground and listened to him, it was clear why.

"The bishops," he said, "side with the wealthy because Rome and the papal nuncio want the church to 'stay out of politics'." Aristide says U.S. interests are Vatican interests, so whatever smacks of anti-Americanism—the attacks on the assembly industries—is branded as political or left-wing or even communist. When Aristide talks about the "expatriation of American profits" and the "new slavery of economic dependence," in other words, he becomes a threat to church and state alike. The Church, after all, has privileges here that are not to be bartered for the people.

He's a very small, very intense man, but not hysterical and not domineering. I had no doubt, as I heard him, that I was in the presence of a holy man who will probably die for Medellin and Puebla and Vatican II and the preferential option for the poor.

As we drove away from his damp, dark dormitory and the tiny classroom and the sparse pharmacy, I saw his name painted on villa walls all over the hills. He has no power, no money, no institutional clout. All he has are the Gospels and the people.

Port-au-Prince is a tragic place. It is paradise on one hand and hell on the other. It sits overlooking the beautiful Caribbean on rolling green hills under the world's bluest sky. And it is a cesspool.

The poor are everywhere; the streets are gullies and the buildings are in various states of collapse. Our four-wheel drive rocked from side to side as we maneuvered from pit to pit on the main streets of town that were so deep they still held the rain water of two days ago.

In the middle of all this sits the USAID building, called by the Haitians, tongue-in-cheek, the "National Ministry of Finance," a gleaming barbed-wired U.S. consulate called "the permanent insult" and a high-walled, perfectly manicured U.S. embassy. There is a sign under the window of the Marine receptionist's office that says "America's Warriors"—as if the U.S. were indeed all the Americas and as if these people who had lived under our occupation from 1915-1934 and from whom they inherited a military dictatorship didn't already know enough about our pomp, our promises, our betrayal and our militarism.

The conversation with embassy staffers was, for want of a better word, sad. They didn't know anything about CBI, the Caribbean Basin Initiative, they said. That's an economic doctrine and they're political attachés. But CBI with its provision for the repatriation of American profits is, in large part, responsible for, or at the very least, contributing greatly to the present political situation here. American businesses pay little or no taxes, provide wages of $3.00 a day and give no benefits. It is the new slavery, a Haitian told us, and this time the "massa" doesn't even supply house, land or protection. These people are free only to starve.

They are trying very hard, I'm convinced, but they're company men who see the policy of the United States with a great deal more clarity than they see the Haitian people and our role in their present situation.

These embassy representatives don't speak Creole and they're short-term staffers trying to give continuity to a foreign policy that changes every four to eight years.

For our part, we want instant and total redress for a situation of long-standing injustice. We want justice, complete justice, and we want it now. Our own judgements are harsh.

It was a somewhat tense but basically civil conversation—they defending American policy, we insisting that they make recommendations for change in it. "Broaden your sources," we said. "Speak the language. Take an interest in Haiti instead of treating it as a necessary stopover on the road to a diplomatic promotion."

"America's Warrior" was still at the reception window when we left the building almost two hours later. And nothing much else had changed either. Good people take such different routes to the same end.

10 pm Monday

After lunch we went out into the city again to St. Martin and Cité Soleil, the slum sections of Port-au-Prince. There was simply no end to the horror.

Cardboard shacks lined mud paths barely more than a car width wide. Children, literally thousands of them, wallowed in the mud and dirt there. The kitchens were burners at the front of the huts, the beds were old mattresses or pieces of cardboard, the roofs were corrugated metal. And there were miles and miles of them. Women washed clothes in basins full of rain water and dumped the suds into open ditches. Starving dogs moved slowly among the children. Men hacked sugar cane and dragged heavy loads on wooden platforms with wooden wheels that were attached to their backs like yokes.

It was human degradation in slow motion. Post-puberty girls squatted against walls to urinate. Small boys had no clothes at all. Women my age had small children crawling all over them or huddled lifeless in the corners of cast-off packing boxes that had delivered the refrigerators of the rich.

The driver of the Land Rover who took us through the area was obviously nervous. I was too thunderstruck to be afraid, too numb to worry about myself, but I put the camera on my lap. I was torn between two values: take film home that would arouse the American conscience or sit quietly and respectfully in the presence of death. After all, what kind of person is it that takes a picture of a corpse? Even in American funeral homes where powders and flowers and chiffons abide, we have not sunk so low that we advertise the clientele in colored photographs.

And here, surely, was living death without benefit of all the niceties. In funeral homes, perhaps, death can be ignored, but here? No, here it must be confronted. And what do you say, American, in the face of this: Hello? How nice to meet you? I'm sorry? I repent? They all looked at us with interest, but no one did a menacing thing. Not yesterday at least. I could hardly promise that much longer.

On the docks of Cité Soleil, the van broke down. We'd gotten out to take some footage of the boats and the laying of nets, but when we went to start the car it was dead. The crowds gathered quickly, all young men and boys, all pushing and asking for money. In Cairo, I had been surrounded by three to five sales boys at a time, all trying to sell cheap jewelry at one hundred times its worth. Here the crowd was 20 to 30 at a time, all wanting something—money, candy, pens, eyeglasses. Anything! Anything at all.

And so, this crowd of nuns and peace people began to give them things. David gave them magic tricks. Helen David gave them sketches of themselves—the kind you pay $25-$50 each for on the Cathedral Square in New Orleans or in the artist's park at Montserrat. Bernadette gave them lessons in the alphabet and I took pictures of them with a video camera. They loved it. And the crowd got bigger and bigger.

As I write these memories and reflections, Haitian radio has been playing the song "Freedom" in the background. Over 80% of the Haitians are illiterate. The radio, then, is very important in this culture, and through this radio everyone in Haiti is being schooled for freedom, while I ride around their island reminding them of their captivity. I wondered what kind of match it would take to light this tinder box.

In the evening, we met with Haitian economists, church leaders and human rights activists to try and make sense of what we'd seen that day. Every lecture was brief but to the point:

• The United States will support corruption in Haiti as long as Haiti remains a security item for the U.S. mainland. And given the fact that Haiti and Cuba share the sea-lane that links the coast of Latin America to the eastern seaboard of the United States, that will surely continue. The goal, of course, is to make certain that Cuba does not attempt to close it on us.

• Free elections and a civilian government endanger American influence and control of the passage, since civilians cannot be counted on to do what the military can be controlled to do.

• The nuncio and the Church in Rome want privilege and a nice peaceful celebration of the 500th anniversary of the discovery of the New World. Since Haiti—where Columbus first landed—is key to that, the Church wants to erase all vestiges of liberation theology here, these leaders believe, to assure a docile show of unity when the spotlights turn this way.

• "Normalization" they call it. What it means is that in the last two years all Church programs that challenged the social structures—literacy campaign, peasant organizing, land reform—have been dismantled.

In fact, Claudette Werleigh, our hostess, has not been with us today because she just got word that the staff of the literacy program she founded has been dismissed for "radicalism." She herself is being given three months "to reflect on her situation," a euphemism, I think, for "get in line," "quit stirring up the women," "quit giving light to those in darkness by teaching them to read," "quit this foolishness called the Gospel." Not here, not now, Jesus; it makes it all so messy.

"What can Pax Christi do?" we asked them, one after another. "Tell the people," they said. "Tell the American people what they are doing to us."

I felt like I'd been here for weeks.

10:45 am Tuesday

We were supposed to leave for Papaye on the Central Plateau at 9:00 am, but changing a battery in Port-au-Prince is not the same as buying a new battery in Erie, Pennsylvania.

It's now 10:30 am and we're still on the veranda and still waiting, but we have to get to Papaye before dark or the danger from roving bands or the Tonton Macoutes is serious. I'm not sure they will be looking for *us*, but they may well be hunting down our activist guides.

9:00 pm Wednesday

We have just ended one of the all-time worst/all-time best days of my life. Dante has never been where I have just been, or there would have been another level added to his description of hell: the non-human, the never human, the pitifully human.

St. Martin and Cité Soleil were a frustration to me. Hinche, the bush and the Central Plateau of Haiti, was a shock in the medical sense of the word—all my systems went into low just to survive.

In the first place, Hinche is 75 miles from Port-au-Prince. It took us over six hours to get there and seven and a half to get back. Every mile out of Port-au-Prince gets worse. The potholes turn to gulleys and the gulleys turn to stones and the stones turn to flowing mud on the edge of a cliff. Houses turn to huts and huts turn to shacks and shacks turn to lean-tos. The trip up the mountain was a progressive, inexorable excursion into dehumanization.

First the toilets went, then the houses went, then the communication system went, and then the water went. It was so methodical. It was all so human.

We were stopped at five military checkpoints along the road. Clearly, the peasants' movement is a great concern here.

We were to have been in Hinche by 1:00. It was almost 6:00 when we got there. It was the rainy season, as well. Most of the peasants who had waited for us all afternoon had already left to begin the 2- to 4-hour walk home before the rains turned the mountains to mud and the darkness doubled the danger.

But the eight or nine who remained were intent on getting their story told. MPP, the peasant movement of Papaye, had started as part of *Ti Legliz*, a basic Christian community of the Haitian church. But the church has put some distance between itself and the more assertive reform movements since the July, 1987 massacre of hundreds of peasants at Jean-Rabel who were organizing land reform actions. What's more, MPP had criticized Catholic Relief Services for its ties with USAID whose policies, they say, are destructive of peasant agriculture.

The movement, they told us, started with two groups. There are now over 5,000 groups with 75,000 members. MPP, in other words, is a factor in the country, to church and state alike.

Their faces were black, black and strong and soft and beautiful. They had been jailed and tortured and terrorized, they said, but they will not stop. They would rather lose their lives than stop. "If the government gave me 2,000 gourdes, I would not quit the movement," one man said. "The money would disappear, but the movement gives my life life. They can kill me but ten more will rise to take my place." We sat in the large steel structure that they call "The

Center" and that we call a storage building in the States. We talked for hours as the sun went down and lightning filled the sky.

They talked about how the movement had taught them to organize, and given them a credit union, and begun reforestation programs to replace resources, and brought them human support. "Before," they said, "people didn't get married because they couldn't afford the wedding reception; they lost everything they had trying to pay for the funerals of their children, but now we all help one another." I thought of the days of Dickens' England and Hugo's France and the days of the Molly Maguires in the United States and knew that, indeed, these people would not quit.

There was only one woman in the group, one of the wives, I thought, a kitchen worker perhaps. And then, as the night got darker and the small, bare yellowish bulb above our heads lost its strength—just when I thought the long, long meeting must be over—she began to speak. And she wasn't shy. "The movement started with three women's groups and now there are seven hundred, 20% of the MPP groups. The movement is good for women, too," she announced. "Men use women like brooms. When they're worn out, they just throw them away." I winced at the image. I had seen their dry, old palm-frond brooms standing beaten in corners. And I had seen dry, old women standing dull and sullen on the mountain roads, as well, all used up, too, and thrown away. "We want equality and dignity," big concepts for a peasant. "We want the beatings to stop. We want men to stop leaving the women and children at home without food while they go out and spend the money."

Her voice got clearer and firmer. I watched the peasant men watch her. "Women's rights will benefit the whole family, but when women made claims, the bishops would repress them. Some women were also jailed. But the movement is bearing fruit: women are speaking out and I have seen women interpret the Gospel at Mass." This universal voice of women is one great common cry of pain, I realized. I looked at her and smiled. She smiled back. But inside I was crying and so, I think, was she.

The building where we were meeting was a public school that had been open for a year and then abandoned as the state has abandoned all social programs in Haiti. The grass around the building was eight feet tall. The outhouse was overgrown and full of animal droppings. The residence halls—six dormitories around a center courtyard thick with high grass and brambles—were standing wide open, doors akimbo and locks broken. There were sinks and toilets and showers, but none of them, not one of them, worked. They were bone dry and full of a year's dirt. A huge tarantula was in the doorway of the dorm; a smaller one was in the cupboard.

It was the worst living condition I had ever been in, and it had been prepared especially for us and with pride.

We strung our mosquito netting together, telling jokes, laughing, sharing bug sprays. I found myself, strangely enough, thinking of all those military checkpoints where they had insisted on knowing where we would sleep that night and thinking, too, of Jean Donovan and Ita Ford and Maura Clarke and Dorothy Kazel. It is astounding how average people like all of us can manage to get into situations like this. It is even more astounding that simple people like these peasants cannot get out of them.

Morning couldn't come early enough for me. I lay and waited for dawn, hungry and dehydrated and apprehensive. I was hoping for better at breakfast.

Women in the kitchen were washing dirty plastic dishes in pans of dirty water. Eggs were cooking in dirty pans over charcoal burning in a washtub. The coffee was being strained through cloth. I realized that I didn't really have an appetite at all. I was too full of North American expectations to eat what two-thirds of this hungry world calls a feast.

We met with the bishop of Papaye who clearly recognizes the conditions of the peasants, the tragic history of the people, the plight of the nation. But he says that the greatest problem confronting the Church in Haiti is "the criticism of the bishops' conference" and that the role of the bishop is "to be neutral because in the same church are people who are both very far right and very far left." I told him I could genuinely understand the institutional implications of that but that the Church also said that we have an obligation to see the world through the eyes of the poor and to respond from the perspective of the Gospel. "How," I asked, "does the Church in Haiti reconcile those two dimensions of the church, the institution and the preferential option for the poor?" And with masterful Church-ese, he managed to talk for over an hour and avoided answering the question. He's a good man, on the side of the peasants, they say, but intent on making sure that "the Church does not take over the role of the state." In the meantime, there are two very distinct churches operating in Haiti: the institutional church and the "church *populaire.*" It will take great saints to walk the tightrope between the two. But if someone doesn't, one or the other will surely be lost.

Outside the bishop's house, in the mud ruts of the city, starving dogs moved among starving children, to snatch pieces of meat at the town butchering block. Crowds circled the car with their hands open and their eyes sad while I turned away with my own. A full-breasted girl of about sixteen bathed under a trickle of water at a public fountain and the whole city squatted in the dirt, like a huge junk yard, selling things that we would not give away to the Salvation Army.

The bone-jarring trip down the mountain was even harder than going up had been. It was market day and burdened beasts and burdened people were walking for miles. We stopped to pick up a young couple who were carrying an infant under an old umbrella in the blazing sun. Judging from where they got on and where they got off the back of the truck, they were in for at least a four-hour walk, a not unusual trip, the Haitians told us.

The rains came early and slicked the shale roads. At the foot of each hill, water ran over the road up to the tailpipe of the van. Whole families gathered to wash their clothes and bathe their children at the waterfall where the road was supposed to be.

There are six months of rain and six months of dry weather in Haiti. During the rainy season, the roads are covered every day, and walking the mountain is both dangerous and impossible. During the dry season there is no water in the area at all. The peasant really never wins. Flat land in the valleys and plains belongs to the rich. The mountain sides with their erosion belong to the poor who walk their crops down in the rain and up in the heat.

We passed lean-to schools where young teachers taught the alphabet in the shade. We watched women cooking in the grass. We saw men wearing "Sanibel Island" T-shirts and walking barefoot on the rocks with bleeding feet. Then, when we got the flat tire, a kind of poetic justice aimed at people in big cars who drove up and down mountains scattering donkeys and women and children, we stepped out of the van into mud over our shoes. Mountain mud, I discovered, is one of the great levelers of life.

They came out of their little one-room shacks to stare or to pose for pictures or to ask for money. It was hard to tell who was the sideshow of note: the peasants and their nothingness or ourselves and our obscene affluence. Surely somewhere there is a middle point. The ideal is certainly not that no one should be rich but, just as surely, no living being should be this poor.

It wasn't long before we began to notice little differences in the ticky-tacky houses with their skewed doors and rotted roofs and small, dark, single rooms—a splash of paint here: "How pretty"; a touch of bric-a-brac there: "How quaint." Then, a little while later, we hardly noticed them at all. How quickly we adjust to the unthinkable.

It was dark when we got back to "Foyer Solidarité," dirty and muddy and running with sweat. The 50-step walk up to the room was the most inviting thing I'd seen in months. When I opened the jalousie window in our little room that night, I was thinking only of the people who were still and forever up at the top of those mountains.

It occurred to me that 80% of the people of Haiti are illiterate. If the same proportion of people in the United States were illiterate, it would mean that not one person in 40 of our 50 states would be able to write and read their own name. Now who do you think would have the money and the cars and the power?

9:00 pm Thursday

We criss-crossed Port-au-Prince all day long, meeting with officials of Caritas, the social service arm of the Catholic church, with officials from the Office of Justice and Peace, with organizers of the fledgling Pax Christi group, with Catholic Relief Services, with past and present operators of Radio Soleil, the Catholic radio station that led the opposition to the Duvalier government and so was closed down twice. Now, though, Radio Soleil is obviously in turmoil. The directors have fired 25 people for "breaches of discipline," and those 25 intend to set up a rival communications system. It is just one more instance of a divided Church in a country where the Church and the military are the only two stable institutions. "But if the Church refuses to take the side of the poor and sides by silence with the privileged, then who shall speak for the people?"

Clearly, the Church itself is in a state of internal turmoil in Haiti, but at one level they all speak with one voice, they all say the same thing: "America, listen to Haiti. Your search for cheap labor and paying markets for your surplus is killing us." And, I thought, it is killing Americans, too. It is easier to open a new plant in Haiti than to continue one in Virginia or Pennsylvania or Michigan. So corporation moguls, with more eye for short term profits then for long term effects, rape without restraint a whole people, a whole culture, a whole nation, and in the process prostitute the morality of our own.

Our Haitian guide was fond of repeating the axiom, "We see from where we stand." Well, the wealthy property owners and the papal nuncio all live on a mountain high above the squalor and the struggle of the city below. What can these good people really see?

"Haiti means business," the brochure from the Department of Tourism and Industry says, and indeed it does: American business. Mean business.

On the final afternoon of the study tour, I drove around the city taking some final footage for the Pax Christi film. Camions, huge trucks that stood people on opposite sides of a wooden divider for the grueling, open-air, stand-up trip to the mountains, lumbered, one after another, out of the city.

Men strained to pull the wheel barrows once dragged by mules or teams of oxen until the government outlawed pack animals on city streets. Now, it is said, the men who rent such liveries to earn their living hauling other people's goods up the hilly terrain die within five years of starting to haul. Women with whole baskets of watermelons on their heads carried children in their arms, the poor clogged the streets, and in a small hospice directed by an American priest and former associate director of Pax Christi USA, Sebastian Muccilli, infant orphans, chronically ill children and a ten-year-old feral girl found in the mountains subsisting on garbage, all wait to die. And no one cares.

The state doesn't provide a cent for the work. The Church says its purpose is to lay out principles, not to get involved with programs. Tourists on cruise liners eat their way across the Caribbean and never even notice this little starving place, except, perhaps, to blame the victims for being lazy, ignorant and inept.

2:30 pm Friday

On the way to the airport this morning, children in droves rushed to the car to sell trinkets or to wash windows or to wipe down the car for a penny here or a bite of food there. And the tap-taps, those brightly-painted little flatbed trucks with their slatted sides and blinking lights that haul people like cattle in lieu of public transportation, drove by sporting their pathetic little names: *Confiance en Dieu*, - Confidence in God; *Merci, Jésus* - Thank you, Jesus; *Esprit* - Hope; Golgotha.

White tourists, as few as there were, left Haiti carrying straw baskets, wearing straw hats, brandishing bright-colored paintings from a drab, dark world. And, as we circled Miami, each of us from our immigrant backgrounds of poverty and oppression, I knew with an awful awareness that the Statue of Liberty had turned out her light.

13
Peace Is Worth Getting Riled About

An interview with Sister Joan Chittister, by the editors of *U.S. Catholic.*

Q: If you had a choice between working for world peace or peace in your neighborhood, which would you choose?

A: There's no such thing as a choice anymore—if there ever was. Perhaps when I was a child in the early 40s, I could have made a better case for ignoring the world outside of my neighborhood. My parents and I drove from Pittsburgh to DuBois, Pennsylvania, for our annual vacation, and I thought of the trip as a major undertaking. And as for flying across the country or jetting across the ocean or even phoning overseas—well, no one I knew had ever done it. In those days, I looked at my neighborhood as the center of the universe.

In the early 1940s, we didn't have television yet, either. Even during World War II, people learned about the war mostly from reading newspapers and listening to the radio. It was only in the 1950s that I could sit in the living room and watch war victims being killed during the 6:00 news.

We Americans live in a new world today. You didn't create it, nor did I; yet we're trying to act as if we lived another, more innocent period of time. At the same time, the whole Christian tradition opposes this isolationist attitude.

Look at the Psalms, for instance. Whenever you pray the Psalms, you are praying for local, national, and global peace. That's because the psalmist wasn't just concerned about the neighborhood or the king; the psalmist prayed for the world at large. As a Benedictine, I pray and study the Psalms every day and, in fact, use them as a model for prayers for peace. If you steep yourself in the Psalms every day, you won't be satisfied with a view of peace that excludes the world outside your neighborhood.

Q: What could I—as only one person—do for world peace today?

A: Do you own a postcard? You could send it to your legislator and ask about his or her voting record on nuclear disarmament. Ask a question or two—that's one of the most subversive actions you can take. You might want to ask, "Why are you voting this way? Why with my tax money? Why are you putting my children and yours in danger? Why are you threatening our planet?" And don't disregard the power of conversation. One honest question or statement can bring a cocktail party to a screeching halt.

As long as people can discuss a subject, they can conceive of doing what they are talking about. But once you say, "No, talking about the best way to win a nuclear war is not discussable in my presence," you've already made a step toward peace. The most current, in-depth research available indicates that there is a great social power when even one person says, "No, I object."

We Americans talk very eloquently about personal freedom and rugged individualism, yet when was the last time you heard someone speak the truth at great personal risk?

Q: Isn't part of peacemaking just keeping the conversation open?

A: That depends on the conversation. When bureaucrats discussed the best way to transport Jews to Germany so they could be gassed, it didn't matter in one way whether they came up with the "right" solution or not. Just to discuss the situation made it conceivable as a normal, everyday activity.

In the same way, the stockpiling of nuclear weapons is wrong, and I need to say that it's wrong—not just simply that it's being done the wrong way or costs too much money. And when I point out, clearly and simply, that a particular conversation or activity is wrong, I probably won't be invited back to the next cocktail party. But who knows who else I might have influenced to speak out the next time?

I was in Texas a few years ago, milling about with a number of people before starting my lecture. There was a huge television in the room and all, of a sudden, Ronald Reagan came on and announced with glee that he had just signed a piece of legislation instructing U.S. border guards to shoot anyone coming over the Rio Grande. I heard people around me make comments like "Well, I hate to see something like this happen, but what else can Reagan do, for Pete's sake; after all, you gotta get tough with these people." And at that point I said aloud, out of quiet desperation, "Well, we could give Texas back." And the room went perfectly still, like one of those E.F. Hutton ads.

Q: What stops people from having the courage to speak out?

A: I think there's a natural cultural blindness. It takes a while to see certain harsh realities, and it can be a very painful process. A lot of people didn't want to see what was really happening in Vietnam, for instance, including me. I am very embarrassed to tell you that other people marched and objected to the Vietnam War long before I did; but if they hadn't marched, if they hadn't held a candle to my eyes, I don't know if I ever would have questioned the war at all.

Q: Doesn't peacemaking need to begin in your own home?

A: God's peace must begin in your heart—and in your home. But you can do many things locally for national and world peace, too. Ten years ago, when my community pledged to adopt nuclear disarmament as our community goal, we agreed to write each year the specific actions we would take to bring about nuclear disarmament. As the prioress of the Erie Benedictine Sisters, I have the great privilege of reading every sister's response. One nun has committed herself to participate in the prayer vigils every month at the Federal Building; another nun—a teacher—is producing a year's worth of peacemaking materials for her classroom. Still another sister, who is a nurse, conducts workshops on the effects of radiation. I could go on and on; but, strictly speaking, these nuns work for nuclear disarmament on a local level; after all, they aren't delegates to the United Nations or running on a peace ticket for Congress.

One 75-year-old sister wrote, "I will talk to my brother, Charles, when I am home for Thanksgiving." I read her words and thought, "That's nice, good for her." Then I read what she wrote in the parentheses: "My brother, Charles, is a retired colonel in the U.S.

Air Force." It's one thing to go to the Pentagon; it's another to go to your brother Charles' home at Thanksgiving, eat his turkey, and tell him that you don't like what he's been doing. Now, that's Christian risk at the local level!

I'm not saying that everybody should march in the streets; though if we did, I think this country would end the arms race much faster. That's how Americans ended slavery and the Vietnam War, and that is how we built up the labor movement. But God doesn't call everybody to make public demonstrations, just as not everyone in medicine is called to do brain surgery. Once I decided to learn how to see the world with the eyes and mind of Christ, I found that working for world peace came surprisingly easy.

Q: Why?

A: I began to see how much Christ loves everyone, and then slowly I started to feel the same way. I couldn't stand it when I saw or read about anyone's life being threatened or destroyed, and it didn't matter where in the world that person lived.

In the Acts of the Apostles, Peter tells his disciples after his meeting with Cornelius, "I have discovered that God's graces are for everyone. I know now that all other people are as human and as much loved by God as I am." Peter had learned to see as Christ sees. And, inevitably, he welcomed Gentiles into the early Church.

Q: How does someone learn to see as Christ sees?

A: It is a continual process. Benedictines read the Scriptures every day and reflect on how to relate them to the modern world. That has been a very, very important part of learning to see through Christ's eyes for me. I read the Gospels and notice how Christ treats the outcasts and listen to how he responds to the social questions of his day.

Some of the questions are variations of those we humans face today. Is AIDS a curse from God? Well, a man asked Jesus about a blind man, "Rabbi, who sinned? The man or his parents?" And Jesus said, "Neither. This man was born blind so that God's glory could shine forth in healing him." Those words tell me that Christ looks at sickness as something to heal, not to use against a person. Then I ask myself, "Well, who are the outcasts of my day and what is my attitude toward them? What are the major social concerns of my world, and how might Jesus respond to them?"

At that point, I begin to study the questions in my world and then try to see them as I believe Jesus would. Many of the issues today are different, of course, because modern technology gives people options that were unthinkable 2000 years ago. Who could have conceived of nuclear weapons or the need for nuclear disarmament in Jesus' time?

I have also this little private theory that may work only for myself, but I like to use it. I imagine I won't die until I've had an opportunity to live all of the dimensions of the human condition as presented by Scripture. And, for instance, when I feel a terrible anger about something, I'll say to myself, "Well, which Scripture am I living now?" And sometimes I find I'm living out the story of Samson. Then I have a choice to make, just as he did. Am I going to pull the ceiling down on myself as well as on all these other people, as Samson did? If so, what have I proven, what have I accomplished?

Q: How important is prayer?

A: Without it I would burn out. I pray to find the will of God and then to do it. I pray to be converted, to be changed—so that I can know God's will and do it. Without daily prayer, my struggle, for peace would be very short, and I'd soon have very little reason to take another step, because often what I set out to do simply doesn't work—at least not on my terms. I may have expected to persuade thousands of people to march in the streets for peace, for instance; but maybe God intended for me to influence only one other person. So without prayer I quickly lose my perspective. Prayer helps me to remember that God doesn't necessarily ask me to succeed in my efforts, just to make them.

Q: Is prayer by itself ever enough?

A: Maybe if I'm on my deathbed and that's all I can do, prayer by itself is enough; but otherwise, prayer without action leads to spiritual complacency or quiet despair. To assume, for instance, that God would never allow nuclear weapons to be used is to completely ignore God's wonderful sense of humor. God has let a lot of things happen in history that you or I would have given even God a D-minus grade for. To rest upon the assumption that God will save us from ourselves is, in my opinion, to sin against our free will.

It has been said that prayer is meant to afflict the comfortable, not to comfort the afflicted. My prayers should get me into the world to make it better; the thought that my prayers are meant, instead, to be the crowning delight of my day is a joke. Christ rises from the dead and tells his followers to look for him in Galilee—not in Jerusalem, the center of power, but in Galilee where the poor are—out in the back country, in the mud.

If God means prayer to be the highlight of a person's day, why didn't any miracles happen when people were praying with the high priests in the Temple? Why instead did Jesus perform most of his miracles among huge crowds of hungry, tired people?

Q: I've always heard that contemplation is the highest form of prayer.

A: If you count on contemplation to help you relax, then what I'm going to say will sound heretical. There is a form of contemplation done strictly for its own sake, but I consider it a form of complacency. In Scripture, God never allows humans to escape into the pure contemplation of God. Moses starts to go toward the burning bush, but God stops Moses short and sends him to deliver the Israelites from Egypt. At the Transfiguration, when Peter wants to set up three tents and stay a while, Jesus simply takes him and the other two apostles down the mountain; and who is waiting for them but a man possessed by a demon, a man who needs deliverance.

Like prayer, real contemplation always points to action and change. Look at the late Thomas Merton, for example. He lived as a Trappist monk, and yet he has more of a social and political effect on people today than any other religious person of our time—except maybe Daniel Berrigan, who is also a poet and contemplative priest.

Q: What is the greatest risk you've taken for peace?

A: My greatest risk came as a Benedictine when I decided in 1978, along with the rest of the community, to work for nuclear disarmament. Believe me, ten years ago especially, few Catholics wanted to see a bunch of nuns standing at the Federal Building, marching with placards in their hands every First Friday. Imagine how you might have felt ten years ago if a nun in your local parish was jailed as a peace demonstrator, and you'll have some idea of the reactions we faced then—and even, to some extent, still face today.

For the last ten years, the Erie Benedictines have also given 10% of all our fund-raising projects to other peace groups in the country because we have wanted to avoid the possibility of—even subconsciously—building a peace monument to ourselves. Now, when I talk about 10%, I mean 10% of all our money. Oftentimes, money that we need to pay the bills goes to other peace groups, but somehow we find other money to live on. For years, we lost benefactors who told us they wanted nothing to do with our community ever again because of our decision to work for nuclear disarmament. We have risked our reputations and our financial resources to follow our consciences.

Q: Was it necessary for all the Benedictines in your community to adopt the same goal?

A: Well, why enter a religious community in the first place? Obviously, you could pray or teach or help people without joining a convent or a monastery. People join so they can worship together in ways they could not possibly worship alone. The community must stand for something, be something together.

In the early 60s, the Second Vatican Council sent all the religious communities back home with instructions to rediscover the spirit of their founders and to determine how to reflect the founder's spirit in a contemporary and realistic way. When the Erie Benedictines went through this process, we came face-to-face with the whole question of peace. Benedictine monks wrote "Pax" over the doorways of every one of their great monasteries in Europe, and they had always protested against the wars in Europe. The Benedictines even helped set the rules and limits of warfare, which were adhered to in Europe for centuries. Even our motto, "Pax," means peace; we've used it ever since the 5th century when Saint Benedict first opened his monastery outside of Rome.

So our Benedictine heritage guided us. Not only that, but we knew we were now living in a time of nuclear warfare that could easily lead to human annihilation.

Q: Are there days when you find it hard to get along with the people you live with?

A: Of course. That's part of being human. It's great heresy to imagine that people need to be perfect to fit into a religious community or a marriage or a parish. By its very nature, a community is made up of broken people who come together. All together, a Christian community makes up a picture of the mosaic face of God. But what do you see in a mosaic but pieces that are very broken? So if each one of us is a tiny peace in God's mosaic, then to exclude anybody from the picture is to begin to destroy one's own spirituality very systematically.

So I take offense at a remark made by one of the sisters in my community; or say the kids are whining, and your spouse snarls. Well, what's so surprising about all that? The people I love the best are sometimes the hardest people to love. Why? Because if you love someone, you are committed to working out your relationship with that person, despite the imperfections on both sides. And that means you inevitably find yourself needing to become more patient, more loving, more honest, just to keep the relationship growing. So in that sense your close relationships are usually the basis for your own deeper conversion to Christianity; and that's not an easy process.

Q: What would you suggest to lay people who don't have a supportive community to fall back on?

A: I would have to say bluntly, "Well, you must find a community" because no one lives the Christian life alone. I think that being a solitary Christian is a contradiction in terms. If our parish doesn't support and encourage your efforts to live an active Christian life, find a parish, or a parish subgroup, that does. Statistics show that many Catholics today do move from one parish to another in order to find a community they can be part of. Christians who work for peace need to find each other; that's why I think Pax

Christi, a national Catholic peace organization, has recently gained so many new members.

Q: Can a family be a spiritual community?

A: Oh, absolutely. I can't think of a stronger witness. And I can't think of a stronger family bond or identity than growing up in a family that builds the sense that each person needs to be involved in something greater than themselves.

My own family, for instance, taught me a great deal about peacemaking, even though my parents never worshipped together or attended the same church. I'm an only child. My father was Presbyterian and my mother was Irish Roman Catholic. I always maintain that I'm the only bona fide ecumenist in most groups because my family and I were able to bridge religious differences before "ecumenical" was a word, let alone a virtue.

I watched my parents struggle against religious prejudice in the church, their families, the neighborhood, the schools, and society in general. And yet they hung on to their marriage and continued to support each other. Maybe that's why now I find it hard to believe that you could present me with any differences that are absolute and unbridgeable.

Q: Are there any parts of the Benedictine rule of your community that might serve as a model of peace for a family?

A: Saint Benedict has a great deal to say to modern-day families, but his writings need to be translated into our modern idioms. His wonderful chapter on humility comes to mind immediately because it is really a chapter all about relationships. How do you live in your world? How do you live with your God? With your children? With the people in your neighborhood or community? How do you live with yourself?

Benedict lived in the 5th century, a century very much like our own. At one point in the chapter, Benedict quotes, "I am a worm and no man." Now you and I don't much like those words today. But what Saint Benedict means is, "Listen. You are not God's gift to the human race, and neither am I. You're just you; I'm just me. And there are other people who have other ideas, other ways, other systems that will work better; but that's okay. The world won't end if you're not right today. Just bring who you are and what you believe, and use it wherever you are today."

So is there spirituality for the family or the laity in that statement? Well, look at our 20th century need to be perfect, to be number one, to get ahead.

In one chapter Benedict says, "There are those among us who say that wine is not a fitting drink for monks; but since some of us can't be convinced of that, try to keep them this side of sober most of the time." Now why did Benedict write such a gentle, human rule? He's confronting the spirituality of the ascetics in the desert—and of any rigid, legalistic person—who would say, "He calls himself a monk with that glass of wine in front of him? She calls herself a nun? They should be so lucky as to lunch on locusts and honey." But Benedict says, "No, all the world around us is good. What we need to learn is how to use the things of the world well." The writings of Saint Benedict are a gold mine; but as I said, they need to be translated.

Q: How do you overcome prejudice when you find it in yourself?

A: Here's a wonderful spiritual exercise that has helped me time and time again. When you go home tonight, sit down and find the most disgusting face you can find on the train, stare at it, and say to yourself, "Now here's the face of God for me." And if you're like me, you'll find that halfway home you're going to say, "This is nuts! It won't work. He smells, and I don't want to get near him. Why can't he get his life under control?" But just keep looking because that's the point at which you've almost got it. Pretty soon you'll know what I'm talking about, because after that, your attitude toward that person and your own life will start to change.

Q: What if I see someone who is obviously very rich, clean and looks very affluent?

A: You can do this exercise with anyone who irritates you—a racist, a punk rocker, or a millionaire who seems insensitive to the rest of us. But first, you must start with the person least like you. The person you least aspire to be. I can aspire to be an affluent professional because I can imagine in some corner of my heart that this would be the perfection of myself, but I do not aspire to be a smelly, dirty street person. But in order to understand who Christ is for me, this is the person I need to see the face of God in. And when you do see God in that person, you'll be able to believe more deeply that God actually loves you. You'll find that you won't need to stand in the back of the church like that man in Scripture and tell God, "Lord, I thank you that I'm not like the rest of these people."

Q: And what do you do when people are prejudiced against you?

A: To begin with, I think I try to be very nonviolent in all my conversations. If someone says to me, "Sister, I want you out teaching my kids, not marching in a peace rally in the street," my job is to listen. I have no right to get angry. At one point in my life I felt the same way as that person. I might try to explain what I am trying to explain today—how I got from there to here. I would try to remind him or her of the days when teaching in a Catholic school was a very radical thing for a nun to do. It wasn't until Kennedy became president that teaching in a Catholic school became an "establishment" occupation for a nun.

I am old enough to have been hissed and booed in the streets of Protestant towns because the people who lived there thought Catholic nuns were subversive. So I might point out that when the vast majority of nuns were teaching in Catholic schools, there were millions of people who thought we shouldn't be.

As Benedictines, we believe that we can get closer to God by looking more closely at things that bother us about other people. For instance, let's say I am irritated by a woman who walks too slowly in front of me when I'm rushing to get to work. Well, this might be a sign that the rhythm of my life is out of kilter. And maybe it would be good for me if I walked a little slower in the morning. If walking more slowly would make me late for work, maybe I need to get up a little earlier.

Q: What can you suggest that might make it easier for people in a parish to work together for peace?

A: Well, I think a parish should take advantage of the spiritual exercises that Catholics already know—like novenas, the Stations of the Cross, the rosary, Benediction, etc.—and show their contemporary applications to peace. What do the Stations of the Cross, for instance, have to do with nonviolence and world peace? That would be a question for the parish to explore.

I just wrote a Marian novena, a contemporary novena called "Mary, Wellspring of Peace," and it was a wonderful spiritual experience. In participating in a community Benediction or the Stations of the Cross, for instance, a parish can help people learn and think about peacemaking from a Christian perspective. There is also a whole generation of people who know what novenas are, and they miss Mary, who is a great peacemaker. Admittedly, there is also a whole generation of younger people who have never experienced a novena; and although they probably will not be able to identify with the mentality of a novena, they will be able to appreciate its content.

In a recent retreat conference, I took the seven capital sins and said to the retreat directors, "What we need to do first is to look at the spirituality we were raised on, not only on one dimension but two: the personal and the global. I know, for instance, that personal pride is my need to dominate others. But isn't pride on a national level also the need to be number one, top of the pack, leader of the world? Isn't that a national deadly sin—a cancer that's eating this country up?"

The materials that a parish presents are also crucial. Wouldn't it be wonderful if during the Marian Year, Catholics all over the country used the Pax Christi holy cards that say "Mary, Queen of Peace" on the front and Pope John Paul II's words "Nuclear weapons are a sin against creation" on the back? Imagine the profound impact of a million of these holy cards floating around this country!

Do you see what I'm saying? Start with what you have in common. Ask parishioners to think about how violence affects them and their families personally as well as people from other lands.

Q: Is there a danger for a Christian in getting too involved with politics?

A: Our American concept of the separation between church and state is debased to the point of the ridiculous. The writers of the Constitution were merely trying to ensure that the United States never has a state-subsidized or state-organized religion. Now, many Americans have stretched the concept of church-and-state separation to mean that nearly every moral issue outside of the family or the parish is solely a "political" question. Is the fact, for instance, that the United States now spends 64% of its entire national budget—and our tax money—on the national defense not an issue for moral scrutiny? In the Old Testament, God often tells the prophets to confront the kings of Israel and Judah with their sins. In our day and age, many Americans would ask our prophets to keep their mouths shut and focus on "spiritual" issues. What needs more moral scrutiny than the nuclear arms buildup?

Someone needs to explain to me why, if the United States is officially religious—"In God We Trust" on every coin of the land—and the Soviet Union is officially and ideologically atheistic, there are no differences in terms of peacemaking between the two nations. Given the proliferation of nuclear weapons, why are we as willing as they are to destroy this globe? In fact, apparently, given the last eight years, why is the United States more willing to blow up the world? The Soviet Union, at least, signed the Geneva Accords and pledged not to blow up the world first. The United States will not sign the same document; we simply refuse to tell other countries that we won't destroy them in a minute if we, as a nation, believe that blowing them up would do us some good.

I would argue that Christians need to speak out on moral issues. A country without a conscience is no country at all. And I believe that all the people of the earth who believe in God—I don't care what their religion is—share a common concern for the earth and see it as a creation of God. No religion denies this fact.

Q: I think many Americans would say that the reason that the U.S. won't sign a certain treaty or other has nothing to do with any intention to blow up the world.

A: I agree; many people would say that. We have a strong sense in this country of being the "Covenanted People of God," the "City on the Hill," the "new Eden." That theology runs very deep in us both as American Christians and as Americans. When I was in graduate school, I did an analysis of the inaugural speeches of every president up to and including the time of Nixon, and I found only one common image running all the way through them, one common Scriptural image in every single inaugural address from George Washington on. Do you know what it was? The chosen people; the Messianic people. Now that was, and in many ways still is, our self image. In other words, we are living the good life, and we deserve to be living it.

But, to begin with, is our country all that happy? Americans just keep getting told that we're living a wonderful life. And I really want to believe that because I want to live a wonderful life. But where is it? Occasionally, someone who can't understand why I protest will say, "Your problem is that you don't love America." But my problem really is that I do love America; I really do. I'm not not-American. I want America to be what they told me it was when I was a little girl. I find it very painful to live in a period when president after president has lied—and lied at the global level and lied very seriously.

Q: Do you think nuclear weapons might currently be preventing a war?

A: Even if you believe that some nuclear weapons can be justified, how many are enough? According to physicist Stephen Hawkings, we now have enough nuclear weapons to destroy every child, woman and man on the planet 10,000 times. Now, if you want to blow up the globe, isn't once enough? If you're so sure that being able to blow up the world is what defends you, how many times do you need to be able to do it to be able to sleep at night?

Somewhere we've got to say, "Enough, stop." We humans are simply stuffing our barns full of poison, full of evil, full of the demonic, and all for nothing—unless we want to use it.

Now many people can't imagine that anyone would deliberately use any of the nuclear stockpile because each major power, they claim, checkmates the other. Although I seriously question this point of view—Hitler, after all, came to power in a democratic society—I'll even grant it. Let's assume for the moment that no insane or power-hungry person will ever come to power and be able to use nuclear weapons. Nevertheless, even given that dubious assumption, there is still room for accidents. Consider the pathetic displays of high technology we've been seeing in Libya and the Persian Gulf recently.

Q: Isn't it too depressing to dwell on the fact that the world may end tomorrow?

A: Yes, it is. I can't go around believing that either. I think it's a Buddhist monk who says, "If I knew that the world would be destroyed tomorrow, I would plant an apple tree today." You know, hope is the virtue of thinking that even I can be converted— that even I can change so anything can change. That's my hope. There's nothing morose or despairing about reality because it can give me a sense of who I must be, how I must act at this period of life. I'm responsible for those weapons. God didn't create them, people did. And people can also uncreate them. That's our task; that's our responsibility.

14

The Spirituality of St. Benedict

There's an ancient story that may best explain the gift of Benedictine spirituality to the modern world. The story says that once upon a time, some seekers from the city said to the local monastic, "Help us to find God."

But the monastic said, "No one can help you there."

And the disciples demanded, astonished, "Why not?"

And the monastic said, "For the same reason that no one can help the fish to find the ocean."

When Benedict of Nursia wrote his ancient Rule in the 5th century, he did not write a manual of spiritual exercises or a codex of canon laws. The Rule was not an excursion into the occult or the mystical or even the grimly ascetic. The Rule of Benedict was a document designed simply to make people conscious of the God-life in which we are already immersed. The Rule of Benedict set out to make the normal and the natural the stepping stones of the holy.

Benedictine spirituality, then, rests on six basic elements that have real meaning in our own time: Prayer, *lectio* or reflective reading of Scripture, community, balance, humility and stewardship of the earth.

Never before in history have those elements been needed more.

Benedict teaches us to this day that prayer is more than the recitation of prayers of petition. Prayer is the putting on of the mind of Christ so that we learn to see the world as God sees it. Benedictine prayer is not designed to change God or to coax God to save me from my selfish self. No, prayer in the Rule of Benedict is designed to change me, to open me to the in-breaking of the Spirit, to stretch me beyond my own agendas to take on the compassionate heart of Christ.

Lectio, or the reflective reading of Scripture that Benedict mandates for the serious Christian, is meant to make me see that the Scriptures were written for me, to me, that my own life is an Exodus story, a salvation story, a crucifixion story, a resurrection story and that as the cycles of my life change, I become a different character in each of the scenarios. I have known what it is to be Esther and not use my influence to save the poor who depend on me. I have known what it is to be Samuel, to be called and called and called and not recognize the Voice. I have known what it is to be Mary and to be rejected for doing what the will of God demands of me now.

Lectio, in other words, gives me understanding and energy and promise.

For Benedict, community was the place in which we work out our own responsibility to continue the task of creating a just and gentle world. "Whose feet shall the hermit wash," St. Basil asks. Benedictine spirituality calls us to bear with one another and hold one another up and call one another to growth and so become whole and holy ourselves.

To a complex world, the Rule of Benedict brings balance and simplicity. In the face of a complex world with its 24-hour work days and constant motion, the Rule asks for a life that deals with a little bit of everything in proper measure: work, prayer, solitude, relationships. The Rule, in other words, is an antidote to excess and to human dwarfism. A proverb says, "Wherever there is excess, something is lacking." The Rule of Benedict mandates a measured life.

The Rule of Benedict says to our times, too, that arrogance is destructive of the human spirit and, in our case, of the country itself. Humility is the quality that calls us to let God be God in our personal lives and to take our proper place among all the creatures of the earth. Humility says that to hold the world hostage to nuclear weapons when we need food and housing and medical care and negotiation is arrogance raised to the point of high art.

The call to "treat all things as if they were the vessels of the altar" is the call to steward the earth, to treat it reverently, to hold it in loving hands. It is the call to keep what is usable, to care for what is vulnerable, to safeguard what is fragile on this planet. It is the call to preserve the environment and to clean our houses and to stop pollution. It is the call to save the earth for our children.

The 21st century is indeed a Benedictine century. We need stability in relationships, creation rather than destruction in the works we do, a Christian attitude toward life and balance to match the frenetic pace of our personal lives, our family lives and our national lives. Benedictine spirituality offers all of that and more.

In one of the ancient monastic stories, it is told that a preacher went from place to place shouting, "We must put God into our lives. We must put God into our lives." But an old monastic said, "Oh, no, not true. You see, God is already in our lives. Our task is simply to recognize that." That's what the spirit of Benedict of Nursia offers to our times.

15

Future of Benedictine Women

The Sufi tell a tale that may have a great deal to say about the future of religious life. The story is about a flowing stream that ran into a desert.

This stream, the story teaches, worked itself across the country for ages and experienced little difficulty. It ran easily around the rocks and quickly through the mountains. No obstacle, it seemed, was too much for this fresh and life-giving water. Then, suddenly, it arrived at a desert. Just as it had crossed every other barrier, the stream tried to cross this one, but it found that as fast as it ran into the sand, its waters disappeared. After many attempts, the stream became very discouraged. It appeared that there was no way it could continue the journey.

Then a voice came in the wind. "If you stay the way you are, you cannot cross the sands. In fact, you will only become a quagmire. To go further, you will have to lose yourself."

"But if I lose myself," the stream cried, "everything I have ever been will be lost."

"Oh, on the contrary," said the voice. "If you lose yourself, you will become more of what you were meant to be than you ever dreamed."

So the stream surrendered itself to the hot, drying sun. And the clouds into which it was formed were carried by the raging wind for many miles. And once it crossed the desert, the stream poured down from the skies, fresh and clean, and full of the energy that comes from storms.

Religious life in the Benedictine tradition is a long-running stream which has watered every period of history, true, but which has also in the process met a number of deserts to which it was required to adapt. Benedictine life has had to change many times in order to remain the same. Benedictine monasticism has, as a matter of fact, been able to adapt to every major change in Western history: the rise of urban centers; the development of the university system; the period of exploration and development. Some of its most active figures, Lioba, Walburga, Benedict, Gregory, Boniface have been recognized as its most contemplative and some of its most cloistered, Bernard, Hildegarde, Gertrude, Mechtilde, its most active. And, as a result, one thing has never dimmed: the value and the vibrance of the life itself.

Well, Benedictinism and all of religious life in general is back at the brink of a desert again. Here at this place, history is a challenge but not a comfort. Eighty-five percent of the religious orders founded before the year 1500 have ceased to exist. Sixty-six percent of the religious orders founded before the year 1850 have ceased to exist. And in our own time, 25% of all the religious of the world—including those of our own monasteries—have left religious life. If religious life is meant to be leaven and light, clearly the yeast is not being recognized; the light is not clear.

The question is why? These are great traditions and good women and true values and tested works. Why wouldn't the world respond in this century to those truths as they did in the last century? The answer, I fear, may be that religious life is not now leavening what the world sees as having gone flat. The answer, I fear, may be that religious are not now shedding light into what the world experiences as darkness.

When lands were barren and chaos reigned, Benedictine life brought agriculture and order.

When the poor roamed in droves and illiteracy crippled the continent, Benedictinism brought stability and education.

When new worlds opened on the backs of outcast immigrants, Benedictinism brought both the faith and the institutions that gave identity and human dignity.

The question for Benedictine women of our time is simply: What is Benedictinism bringing through us to this world today? In a period of massive social change, is there apparent in us any reason beyond ourselves to exist? Or has Benedictine life become only the remnant of a previous Gospel world, rather than the bright light of the Gospel in our own times? Who looks to our monasteries for solace, for support, for spiritual sustenance? Who comes to our monasteries, the rich or the poor? Most of all, what do people see when they look there: a monasticism of past ages or models of meaning for our own age?

Today's Issues

Three issues, I believe, lay special claim to Benedictine values in this shifting century:

• Globalism: the notion that those who starve in Africa while our barns are full of wheat have claim on our conscience;

• Nuclearism: the notion that massive evil can be permitted in the name of resistance to evil; and

• Feminism: the notion that women are both as graced and as gracing as men.

And it is these issues that may well determine the future of Benedictinism, as well as the future of the world.

The *Dialogues of Gregory* recount that "Benedict saw the whole world as in a single glance." In our time, too, unless we can see the global as local and the local as global, we may be seen as pious people, perhaps, but not as Gospel people. We may be seen as sincere religious, but never as saintly religious. It is hard to imagine how we can pray the Psalms or read the prophets with all their cosmic dimensions day after day and do nothing as communities to confront the policies of our own world which create those same sufferings today—the exploitation of Third World workers, the lack of human services, the legislation that favors the rich and abandons the poor, the government budgets that ignore the widow and the orphan. How is it possible to be Benedictine and ignore the Instruments of Good Works that cry for doing in our own day? How is it possible to be a Benedictine whose hospices for pilgrims and poor at one time covered the continent with security and now be concerned only that the mass migrations of our own time do not upset the routine of our days?

In a world where the best resources of the time—human, financial and physical—are expended on the tools of human destruction rather than on the mechanisms of human development, how is it possible to preach Benedictine peace and say nothing about the growing threats that come to the survival of the planet from those who design and develop and deploy nuclear weapons or nuclear thinking? How is it possible to be a member of the Order that saved civilization and never so much as send a postcard of protest to the makers of nuclear weapons, let alone preach the politics of peace?

In a world where two-thirds of the illiterate, two-thirds of the poor and two-thirds of the hungry are women, how is it possible to be a credible Benedictine woman and never do a thing to change such a system, rather than simply attempt to repair the wreckage it leaves? How is it possible that Benedictine women, who are among the best-educated and best-organized women of the world, are heard so little and so seldom and so weakly on the exploitation and exhaustion of half the human resources of the world, women?

Future Credibility

If Benedictine life for women is to be credible in the future, it will have to begin quickly to draw on the strengths of the past, rather than the listlessness of the present. It is not that we failed in the last century. It is precisely because we succeeded so well that it is time for change again. The tasks of the 19th century are over. It is the tasks of the 20th to which we must bring the wisdom of a life lived in Scripture, community, stewardship, hospitality and mutual service. It is not the problems of the present that will destroy us; it is our unwillingness or our inability to confront them with the flaming fire of the Gospel life.

There are obstacles, of course.

In the first place, we are deeply entrenched, most of us, in the ministries and institutions of the past. But it is also true that we can use those very schools and hospitals and lands and facilities and guest houses and chapels and publications and spirituality centers to speak truth to the tenor of our times—to call for justice as well as charity. It is not enough for us to have institutions that are viable. The institutions that we have must also be truly prophetic, not simply agents of the state. In Israel, when the prophets of the court said only what the king wanted to hear, they neither grew nor prospered, nor was Israel renewed on their account.

Indeed, our communities will be smaller in the future than in the past if for no other reason than that entrance rates and death rates are not in balance. But size is no measure of the vibrancy of the ministry. Religious life is called to be a leaven in the world, not a labor force. It is what we are about, not how many of us who are about it that will be the measure of our meaning.

The theology of religious life has become unclear. The whole notion of the radical Christian life has gone by the wayside with the domestication of Christianity in the Western world. Exaggerated and excessive individualism has marked religious life, as well as society, to such a point that personal piety has become a poor and meager substitute for the Gospel life, the life that witnesses and proclaims and models the reign of God. Here. Now. In such a world, religious life becomes a way of living instead of a way of life, and customs and institutions rather than heat and light become the standard and the norm.

The great abbeys of the early Middle Ages spoke convincingly to their times about the possibilities and practices of their times. They raised great schools when schools were few and far between. They developed great liturgy when prayer was barren and remote. They became missionary when social stability broke down. If Benedictinism has been anything, it has always been contemporary. The question is, can the people of our day see the concerns of our day mirrored and met in us or do they simply see in modern monasticism the keepers of the past and a kind of religious removed from real life? But to confront the questions of the time with the standards of the Gospel, as Samuel, Daniel and our foremothers did before us, is to announce the death of decline. Like all the major moments in history, there is no place for anomie and ennui in religious life now. Like the Israelites in the desert who needed new commandments for direction, so indeed do we.

The problem is that in a world that is linked by a single camera, under the threat of destruction by a single trigger, drawing from a single resource pool, and defined only by the male model, no one can with integrity be a refugee from the Gospel anymore.

In every age and every way, Benedictines have given the same values: community in a hierarchical world, humility in the midst of the idolatry of status, obedience where pride and exploitation reigned, and peace in the face of the chaos of sin. Those values have never been needed more.

And how shall we do them? And what shall they mean?

In the first place, we will need the very disciplines that we have needed before, but in fresh, new forms.

We will need the kind of asceticism that models the possibility of living within limits in a world that encourages infinite desire in a world of finite resources.

We will need the kind of stewardship that uses goods for the sake of others.

We will need a commitment to the kind of peace that preserves the planet.

We will need to model and to speak for a community of equals in a world that has been built on inequality.

We will need to be communities of alternative concerns rather than communities of no concerns whatsoever.

It is not numbers of religious that is the agenda for the future; it is the very meaning of religious life that we must be about. It is not the continuation of what we have done well in the past that must be our concentration; it is the cry of the present to which we must attend if we are to be authentic. It is not witness by withdrawal from the great questions of life that will determine our value; it is being "in the world, but not of it"; it is speaking truth to power that is really needed of religious life again for its witness to be valid and its meaning to be real. If the history of Cluny teaches us anything, it teaches that we will not be forgiven our indifference.

How shall we live out Benedictine values today?

Among the Desert Fathers the same question, it seems, was asked centuries ago and the same answer, it seems, was given:

Abba Lot went to see Abba Joseph and said, "Abba, as much as I am able, I practice my little rule, keep all my little fasts, say my prayers, keep the silence, and keep my thoughts clean. What else should I do?" Then the old man stood up and stretched out his hands toward heaven, and his fingers became like ten torches of flame. And he said, "Why not be turned into fire?"

The question of the future is not a vocation question. Because there is no dearth of need, there is no dearth of vocations. God always comforts the people. The only question for us now as we confront this latest desert of our own day is simply, will we or will we not be turned into fire? Fire so bright that young woman can see clearly that to be a Benedictine woman is not to disappear but to be changed by storm into energy, to be turned into fire, to be consumed by light and heat as were the great Benedictine ages before us.

16

A Rule of Life

An interview with Sister Joan Chittister,
by the editors of *Sojourners*

Part I

A Sign and a Choice: The Spirituality of Community

Q: You are part of a tradition that goes back more than 1,500 years, and one of the major aspects of that tradition is the importance of community. Religious life has always taken the shape of community. Could you talk a little about why that is so?

A: It's Basil, a Father of the Church, who says, "Whose feet shall the hermit wash?" That question is the basis for the spirituality of community.

The function of the Christian community in sharing the bedrock of Christian spirituality is the upbuilding, the co-creation of the kingdom; the bringing of the kingdom now, the bringing of the now to the kingdom. So, like the community recorded in the book of Acts, the major witness of the new Christian community is the creation of an alternative way of life.

Benedict of Nursia, founder of the Benedictines, deepened his own spirituality to the point that he had a new vision of the Christian life. He looked around post-Constantinian Rome and saw a well-established, politicized church. It was a church that had been made church by virtue of the baptism of the emperor and his decree that all his subjects would likewise be baptized.

An analogy would be an emperor who was a basketball player decreeing that basketball should be the only sport in the empire. So everybody plays it; but that doesn't make everybody a basketball player. So the emperor decreed that everybody was Christian, but that didn't make everybody a Christian. Benedict was immersed therefore in a "pagan Christian" culture.

Although the Edict of Constantine in 313 liberated Christianity in Europe, it also began the murky merger of the sacred and the secular. And that's been as much a burden as it has been a blessing.

That's the environment which young Benedict of Nursia saw 150 years later in the late 5th century in Rome. He didn't attempt to convert Rome. We have no history of Benedict of Nursia preaching in the streets, approaching the government, or going to Church figures; he simply left Rome to begin an alternative way of living.

He provided a sign and a choice—not an argument or a program. And that sign and choice is the Christian community at the level of a radical dimension of love.

What is the radical dimension of love? It is the sign that strangers can become brothers and sisters in Christ.

And what's the power of this community in 1987? We've never had a more fragmented world, or a more pseudo-nationalistic world, or a more chauvinistic world. And so if monasteries and convents and intentional religious communities are a sign of anything, they're a sign that you can transcend all the differences, all the barriers, all the impossibilities, all the things that people say can't come together.

Monasteries are a collection of all the differences of the world made one in Christ. And that's the nature of communal spirituality. It's reflecting in the contemporary community, in the ongoing Christian community, what was the sign and model of the community of Acts.

Q: Could you say a little more about how communities continue to be signs and models in contemporary society?

A: Any Christian community has within itself the possibility of transcending every institutionalized division against which the world is presently struggling. Economic divisions are transcended in communities with a common purse. Personal differences, meaning ethnic differences, are transcended in common living. Hierarchical differences, differences in power and wealth, are transcended by the creation of a community of equals.

Political differences are transcended in the Gospels. We carry one banner, we follow one Christ, we develop one kingdom. And those are precisely the enigmas and the conundrums with which the present world is dealing. Those who say that Christian community life is irrelevant or out of date may well themselves be irrelevant and out of date. It has never been more contemporary, except maybe when it all started!

Q: Could you comment on the role of prayer in your community specifically, and in the life of any community? How have you developed a spirituality of community?

A: We all, I believe, accept the notion that the function of prayer is not to cajole God into saving us from ourselves. The function of prayer is not magic. The function of prayer is not bribery of the Infinite. The function of prayer is not to change the mind of God.

The function of prayer is to change my own mind, to put on the mind of Christ, to enable grace to break into me. So, if you're going to have a communal spirituality and witness, then you must have a praying community.

The monastic community has a prayer life, developed around what St. Benedict called the *opus Dei* and what the churches traditionally called the "Divine Office," what we now call the "Liturgy of the Hours." It's the speaking of the Psalm life of the people of God for our own time.

The Psalm life has three dimensions: personal, national, and global. The psalmist prays out of the struggles of the psalmist, out of the struggles of the people, and out of the consciousness of the cosmic, of the universal: "All nations shall stream to you"; "You shall see the poor"; "In you are all things." So, this prayer life of a Benedictine monastic community is equally conscious on all levels.

I'm here as an individual intent on contemplative conversion, intent on developing in my life over a period and process of time the ability to see with the eyes of Christ, and to put on the mind of Christ. I'm here as part of a community that claims to be a Christian community, and therefore has to struggle with its interpersonal agendas, with the life needs of one another, with being something other than itself. In order to do something, I have to be something. In order to be for someone else, I have to be part of a group. And then finally, we're here praying out of consciousness for the whole global community, for all the people of God.

To some the notion of monastic life is a phenomenally well-institutionalized narcissism. It is precisely the opposite. If and when it ever becomes that, it's at its most decadent. When monastic life is life only for the monastics, then it ceases to be monastic life. That's the paradox of it. When prayer is privatized religion on a spree, it's not prayer.

What is the contemplative life? In the first place, "contemplation" and "enclosure" are not necessarily synonyms. Enclosed communities are not necessarily called to be any more contemplative than my own community. Enclosure is a vehicle for contemplation. But so is stopping by the beaten person on the roadside.

The oldest mystics that we have in organized religious expression—the fathers and mothers from the desert, the gurus of the Sufi tradition, the masters among the Hasidim—all have similar parabolic insights into contemplation. There is a story about the master saying to the disciples, "Tell me how you know when it is dawn." And one disciple says, "Master, is it when we can tell the fig tree from the lemon tree at 100 paces?" And the master says to the disciple, "No, that is not how you will know it is dawn."

So a second disciple says, "Well then, Master, is it when you can tell the sheep from the goats at 50 paces?" And the master says, "No, that is not how we shall know when it is dawn." Then the third disciple says, "Well then, Master, how do we know that we have seen the dawn?" And the master says, "We will know that we have seen the dawn when we can see the face of Christ in the face of any brother or sister, no matter how near or how far."

That's contemplation. That's the fruit of the contemplative life. And unless you're putting on the mind of Christ, I don't know if you'll ever see the face of the Christ in the other, or the face of the cosmic, or the face of the people of God in the other. You may be a highly-efficient social worker or a marvelously compassionate do-gooder, but you will not necessarily be a Christian contemplative.

Q: Given all you've said about the different ways contemplation happens, how important are discipline and ritual as part of contemplation, particularly in the life of a community?

A: I happen to think it is of the essence. It's profoundly important. Obviously, we don't think a discipline of prayer can be dispensed with; we do it three times a day as a community. That's the essence of the monastic vocation.

I wouldn't argue that every community has to do it as a community. But I would argue that every community has to have a community spirituality, and that it must be regularly ritualized, so that in prayer and liturgy and ritual, we are as able to express ourselves as a community as we would at supper, at Christmas, or in work. Because the spirituality is the bedrock of the community. We have to be formed in a common spirituality not just for the sake of communication, but for the sake of common energy, common values.

In a monastic community, it's imperative for us that as a whole group we call ourselves to spiritual development at least twice, and usually three times, a day; and that we be a place where others can come, knowing at certain times the community will always be in prayer together, and that they have a praying community to relate to as their own lives require it. I can't honestly think that you could have a community spirituality unless that spirituality were communal.

Q: But I've also heard here a great deal of emphasis put on individual spirituality and the recognition that the communal spirituality is made up of individual spiritualities.

A: Absolutely. By communal spirituality and common values, I never mean a "marshmallow mind."

Religious communities, and monastic communities in a special way, are probably the only institution left in the United States in which every generation lives under the same roof. We have sisters upstairs in their 80s who have been in this community for more than 60 years! There is no way that the spiritual life of a 25-year-old can match the spiritual life of an 80-year-old. It doesn't make the

80-year-old's spiritual life better, necessarily. It isn't any more sincere or any more real than the spiritual life of our 25-year-olds.

But a 25-year-old can only have a spiritual life that comes out of 25 years of experience. So she comes in with her own agendas, her own angels to wrestle with, her own ideals, her own questions; and the 80-year-old has long since put those questions down. She has another full set of questions.

We each bring our own questions, our own angels, our own internal wrestlings, and our own special gifts to community prayer and out of community prayer, to be lived in very special ways. We're not talking about a "common mind," we're talking about a "communal mind." And they're not the same thing.

In addition to that, in the Benedictine monastic tradition, preceding and succeeding the communal prayer is also the concept of *lectio divina*, the meditative personal reading of Scripture. What is this Scripture about? And what is it saying to my life? The development of the contemplative mentality comes out of all that. Communal spirituality guarantees the provision of an environment together for growth alone.

Q: One of the things that has most touched me here is the sense of community that exists not only among those of you who are here, and not only among contemporaries in other places, but also with those sisters who preceded you. During the daily prayer, you often pray for the sister who died on this day in 1970, or 1906, or 1862. Being a member of a community with 15 years rather than 1,500 years of tradition, I sometimes envy that sense of history. What does it mean to have the strength of that tradition, what do you feel you draw from it, and what responsibility do you feel toward the generations that will come after you?

A: Well, you've put your finger very, very sensitively on what, for me, and I think for most of the members of this community, is one of the gems of the tradition and a piece of the glue in the house. That is, we pray for two people every single day, and they will be prayed for from now for as long as this community lasts.

In the morning, we pray for the sister who died on this date in any year since our community's foundation in 1856; and in the evening, we pray for the sister next to die. So here you have a custom that very consciously links the great moment of community, the past and the future.

When people ask, "How many are there in your community?" I always say "A little over 300—about 150 of us are in the cemetery, and about 150 of us are at home." Our older sisters have lived with almost all those people, except our earliest founders; but they lived with people who lived with our earliest founders.

So all of that history is very much alive in the house. Why? Because we know who built the buildings that we all live in. And we know who's going to build the next set of buildings that we're going to minister in.

The irony is that this notion of the continuing community through time to the end of time becomes a very strong foundation for change. Because you are continuous, you can change.

Because so many went before you, on such a different path, you are freed to make your own path. Because if they did it, so can you. They survived, so can you. If they were made holy by it, so can you. It's a chain of memories that makes the future possible.

When we were facing renewal in 1970, after Vatican II, we remembered that in 1850 three young women left a monastery in Bavaria that was already 700 years old and came here to start over again. So, that prayer is a prayer of possibility and a prayer of support. Since it's happened to those before us, we will be with those for whom the great light is now. And some day our own great light will come and be appended to that list.

For instance, I entered the community when I was 16, and I've been here now more than 30 years. So in the chapel when we pray for Sr. Pierre, that first sweet, old, wonderful woman who showed us how to do dishes here, she's right there. I remember her.

Sr. Pierre was already a little sunken gnome of a woman by the time I got here, but very bustling, very quick, obviously the cornerstone of the house. She was what in those days was called a "domestic sister." She was a cook, and she did laundry and things of that nature. And she always had a wonderful word for the youngsters in the house.

In those days, the mother superior always put out the assignment book—we called it just "The Book"—on Friday nights. And you rushed home from school on Fridays to check the book on the chapel window to see what you were assigned to do the next week. Was it to wait tables, or to read the Scripture, or to answer the door?

I can remember standing at the book on a Friday afternoon, and I obviously was not pleased with my assignment. Sr. Pierre came by and put her little gnarled arm around me and said, "Now darlin', you be remembering. When you come to the book and ya get what you like, then Jesus give ya a hug. But if ya come to the book and ya get what ya don't like, then Jesus bends right down and kisses ya." When we pray for her in chapel, I say to myself, "Okay, Pierre, I'll try to remember."

Q: It is often said that one of the signs of the health of a community is its sense of hospitality toward others who are not part of a community, and certainly the many times I've visited here I've been overwhelmed by this community's sense of hospitality. I would say that among your many gifts, hospitality is one of the strongest. How does that sense of hospitality relate to your sense of community and spirituality?

A: Well, it's definitely basic to the Benedictine Rule. One of the most widely-quoted phrases from the Rule is the chapter on the reception of guests. It's a very interesting chapter when you consider that, at least in modern minds, the Benedictine life is seen as a basically ascetic, withdrawn, other-worldly mode.

But you cannot find the foundation for that mode in the Rule, which contains an entire chapter on the reception of guests. The chapter begins, "Let all guests who arrive be received as Christ, because Christ will say 'I was a stranger and you took me in.' And let due honor be shown to all, especially to those of the household of the faith and to wayfarers."

Now that's a key line in a 5th-century rule. Nothing was more dangerous than crossing Europe. Benedictine monasteries were the first Holiday Inns of the Western world. It was one of the few places where people could come and sleep well and not have to worry about being mugged, rolled, or knifed in their sleep.

It was a tremendous contribution to the western Europe of the time. You could cross Europe and stay in a monastery of your own tradition every single night, because they were spaced a day's journey apart. So for a Benedictine not to practice hospitality is for a Benedictine not to practice Benedictinism.

It's a very special gift, and I think it has an awful lot to say to our own time. The Benedictine monasteries were among the first to take the sick and the dying into their own infirmaries. Because death in a pagan world was a punishment, there were all sorts of taboos surrounding death. Barbarian peoples left the dying on the sides of the roads. And the monasteries were very, very quick to begin the first hospices, so that these people could die in clean beds in a Christian environment.

The chapter goes on to say, "When therefore a guest is announced, let them be met by the superior and the community with every mark of charity."

Now, what's the application? They're not pests. You don't throw them in a room and ignore them. You make them welcome: "It is good for us that you have come."

The Rule says, "And let them first pray together." This is the Christian community that you've come to. And our first gift is to come down into this consciousness of God with us, so that we can get the most from one another. It's a contemplative encounter, an encounter blessed by the presence of God.

"And then let them associate with one another in peace." We're not here to contend. You did not come to be converted. There'll be no Catholic magic. No attempt to evangelize. No proselytizing. You will simply come as a creature of God, and therefore you must be gift.

"The kiss of peace should not be given before a prayer hath been said on account of satanic deception." That's not necessarily a reference to chastity. It's a reference to the notion of why you are about what you are about. This is not a human act. You're not here because you're a friend or a lover. This is the reception of the people of God to the place of God, in a godly way.

And then the chapter says, "In the greeting, let all humility be shown to the guest, whether coming or going." In other words, no arrogance, no status, no display of pomp. "Welcome to my house." This is hospitality almost in the biblical Middle Eastern sense, meaning you are doing me the favor. I get to give something away. I've been given a great abundance. Now how shall I possibly distribute it, unless you come?

So the function of community is to make community for the other. For those who don't have the opportunity, perhaps, for community. Or for those who are without their own community at this moment. Or for those who think that no community would have them at this moment.

There's another great chapter in the Rule on the abbot's table. It reads, "Let the abbot's table always be with the guests and the travelers." When I was a kid in this community, we weren't allowed to eat with anybody and we weren't allowed to eat out. When we read this, I would think, "Huh, Mother gets to go to all the parties."

When I got older, I discovered what they were really asking of the superior. If you are the sign and symbol of the center of this community, of its environment and its character, its ministry and its fidelity to the Gospel, then you, my friend, shall be the sign of hospitality and community to every person who walks into this house.

And they shall all eat with you. Not in the kitchen, not with the help, not with the novices. They shall be received at your table. You are going to take them right into the heart of the community— the abbot who is the house, the abbot who breaks the bread, the abbot who gives away what the community has to give away. The abbot who says there's no separation here, we don't receive you here as an inconvenience or a stranger. You are here as gift so that we can give.

Q: I think younger communities can learn from your tradition of hospitality. When you're involved in so many activities, as we are at Sojourners, sometimes you want to come home and have home just be home. And welcoming people isn't always easy. But when I come here, I always experience the richness of that tradition and the fact that hospitality is indeed a commitment of every member of this community.

A: There must be some truth in what you're saying, because I've heard it from so many people. One guest summed it up with exquisite artistry. She said, "I always get the feeling when I come to this community that I am everybody's guest. You can't pass anybody in the hall who doesn't say, 'Can I help you?' or 'Do you know where the coffee is? I'll take you there.' "

As I listened to her, I couldn't understand why this was surprising to her. I would just take that for granted. Then I discovered that she is a businesswoman and a single parent; she's always doing for somebody else. And she is basically ignored in the apartment complex in which she lives. She carries the kids and the groceries up and down the stairs without any help. She does all those things that people have to do to struggle through life, and expects to be ignored.

And then she comes to a place where everybody is expressing concern about her comfort. It seems to me, God willing, it does exist here; but if it does, it's because it should.

Q: I think it exists because you don't just receive the guest, you receive each other in a way that says "I care about your comfort. I'm concerned about you."

A: I'm completely convinced that you cannot have hospitality in the community unless the level of community cohesion and concern is high at all times. I have always maintained that the level of your hospitality will be measured by the depth of your prayer. And the depth of your prayer will be measured by the depth of your hospitality.

These three things are sides of a triangle—the members' genuine human concern and affection for one another; their opening that concern to take in the others who come; and the prayer and the Gospel, which are the reason we're doing this.

Q: On one hand, you've said community can't exist for itself because it needs to exist for people beyond itself. On the other hand, I think there is sometimes the temptation among those of us who live in community to see community only as a base out of

which we offer our ministry to the rest of the world. Could you discuss that kind of tension?

A: That's an important question and not easily answered. It touches on a much broader and much more clarifying question of communal spirituality. Let me look first of all at what I clearly know best, which is the history of Roman Catholic communities and spirituality.

In the history of community life in the Roman tradition, we have two types of community spirituality: monastic spirituality and apostolic spirituality. Everything I have said to this point, I would argue, applies to both traditions, but monastic spirituality institutionalizes some of those qualities quite differently than apostolic spirituality.

Monastic life is communal life, and so is apostolic life, to a certain extent. But to the monastic, community is primary, and out of community comes the expression of prayer and ministry. In apostolic communities, ministry is primary. And ministry leads to the formation of community and the development of the prayer life.

Benedictine tradition says that the Benedictine charism is to seek God in community and to respond in prayer and ministry. The apostolic tradition says, "Our function as Christian communities of faith is to serve the people of God in ministry for the upbuilding of the kingdom." I think that is an accurate rendering of how most apostolic communities would state their mission. If you are a monastic, you certainly have ministries. And if you are in the apostolic tradition, you certainly have faith communities, so they're going to erupt in prayer. But the styles of community, the expressions of community in prayer, and even the ministry, may well differ, in order to focus on the basic element.

Community life as it's structured or expressed by a monastic community may not be at all the same as in an apostolic community. For instance, an apostolic order may live in much smaller groups than we live in. Or they may group around their works, where we would group around the community.

We would go to a place to be together, to be a sign of community, and then minister out of whatever gifts were there. An apostolic community may say, "This is a ministry that must be given to these people," and so those people who are capable of giving that ministry would go there. Each of those spiritualities will develop expressions of prayer and community. That's an important distinction to me, in reference to your question.

Your question points to another central question for all of us, which is, does the community exist as a vehicle for my ministry? I would argue that that assumption is false in either a monastic or apostolic community. Even when a common ministry is what draws us into the faith life and community, that does not give me the right to use that group as simply a touchstone for my own work.

The function of community life is for us to be and to do together what we cannot possibly do nearly as well alone. Can you pray alone? Yes, you can. Can you pray better in a group that enhances and is a vehicle for your prayer? Yes, you can. Can you work alone? Of course you can. Will you work with more energy and probably more effectiveness if you're working with a group of similarly-committed people? Yes, I think you will.

Will you be a sign of Christian presence and sense of community alone? Certainly. Will you be an even stronger, clearer, more capable sign of community if you're supported by people who think about community the way you do? Yes, you will.

If you find somebody who thinks that the community exists in order to facilitate their own agenda, they haven't formed their communal spirituality. Communities don't exist, they're developed. And community is developed by community members. When I'm not developing community for you, and I'm simply using what you develop for me as a way to go about my interests in life, I'm not living community. I'm allowing you to create it for me; but I'm not living it.

I only live community when I, too, create community. And that means that you can't be the only person in charge of the guests. It can't be just your responsibility. That's when a community will get ineffective and unbalanced—when some of us expect the rest of us to keep it in existence.

That is not to say that everyone does the same things. Everyone doesn't have to be on hospitality, but we must all be hospitable. Everyone doesn't have to perform the same community task, but every one of us has to perform our community task. Everyone does not have to be responsible for the same things in the same ways, but we must all feel a responsibility for this community. No other sign of community will be authentic.

Q: Your community exudes joy and celebration. How is that related to your prayer life?

A: Let's look at three dimensions of that. A long time ago, the Catholic Church made the distinction between ordinary days and feast days. The Church punctuated the calendar year with feasts. The whole notion was to lift moments of time out of the humdrum for special consideration.

Feast days were very important in early Europe, in an agrarian society that worked so hard from dawn to dark. The peasants and the serfs carried the entire economy on their backs. The feast day was one of the ways that the Church, like the Jews in the observance of the Sabbath, brought equality to the society.

It was a long time before the 40-hour week. But the Church said this great feast is like a Sunday, and therefore you cannot force these serfs to work. So it was free time. It was the first contribution to the labor movement, the first contribution to equality, and it was a profound theological contribution to the notion of hope. It was a sign that the victory had come for some, that life was a great gift.

Now you take the concept of joy in the Christian tradition and you add it to the concept of redemption and salvation, the Messianic prophecy, and you embody it in your life. You're not talking about cocktail parties, you're not talking about organized laziness, you're not talking about shirking your responsibility, you're not talking about being unreal.

How can Christians celebrate? How can peace people celebrate when you are looking down the barrel of a neutron launcher? How can you women possibly be happy when you live in a Church that treats you as if you are less than full human beings? Because the victory has been won. And hope has come. And light has been seen. And some people have shown it.

So it's an absolute theological essential to celebrate. Any religion or any community or any period of history or time that wipes out joy and feast I find very suspect. More neurotic than holy.

Here the Church has been faithful as an institution over time. No matter what warped spiritualities might get hold of the people, the Church has always been a sign of joy and celebration.

Now it's an easy move from that consciousness of the face of joy as a theological necessity to joy in prayer. Prayer is not a discipline. Prayer is a dispensation from the humdrum. Prayer is a chance to take a look at other things.

Prayer is a chance to sit down and reflect on something more important than getting our today's mail. The more sincere a Christian you are, the easier it is to fall into that bear trap, and consequently, to lose a depth of spirituality that's tragic. It's a spirituality that corrupts instead of uplifts. The function of prayer is to give expression to the signs of joy and hope you see. And it's also the place to count your real joys.

Now if joy is theologically necessary, and if it is provided for in its gentlest form in a regular prayer life, then it is clearly apparent in the life of the community. It has to be. You have a right then. It legitimates happiness!

There used to be a marvelous poster quoting Leon Bloy: "There's no such thing as a sad saint." And I believe Thomas Merton said, "Joy is the infallible sign of the presence of God." The celebrating community, then, is the community that rejoices in its Christianity and in the fact that it is community.

Community comes with a genuine respect and acceptance of one another as people. And you celebrate that. And you make it by celebrating it.

Play exposes us as people. Once you have played with all these people, you just treat them so much more gently in their personal lives, in community meetings, in the discussions of who you are as a group. Joy and celebration enable you to keep humanity in mind.

Part II
A Full Picture of God: A Look at Feminist Spirituality

Q: You have been at the forefront of issues dealing with women in the Church, and you've seen the role of women in the Church go through a lot of change through the years. But even though the understanding of ministry for women is changing and expanding, women in the Catholic Church are still denied ordination. How do you think this situation will be resolved?

A: You cannot have a changed understanding of the notion of ministry for women until you have a changed understanding of the notion of the personhood of women. The question is simply, what is a woman for?

And the answer is not from biology. It's from Shakespeare. It's Shylock's answer in *The Merchant of Venice*: "If you prick us, do we not bleed? If you tickle us, do we not laugh? If you poison us, do we not die?" The answer is, "I am fully human. Therefore, I am fully graced by God. Therefore, I am fully called by God."

When they baptize a woman they don't say, "Now we pour this slightly diluted water on this slightly diluted creature who will give us slightly diluted Christianity—or ministry or service—back." When they bring the girl up to confirm her, and she stands next to the little boy who is her peer and colleague in this great Christian moment, they don't tap him on the cheek and say, "You are confirmed to do battle for Christ our Lord and the spreading of the faith," and then look at her and say, "You are almost allowed to do battle for Christ our Lord in faith."

Someplace along the line, the effects of the sacraments are going to have to be able to be manifested in the ministries, as much for a woman as for a man. There's either something wrong with the present theology of ministry, or there is something wrong with the present theology of all the sacraments. If women qualify for baptism, confirmation, salvation, and redemption, how can they be denied the sacrament of ministry?

Q: Could you talk about how women coming to that understanding of their personhood and their ministry are changing the way the Church looks at spirituality?

A: The interesting thing about the Church is that its spirituality is basically very feminine. Look at what psychiatrists and psychologists tell us are basic masculine traits or values or qualities and what are basic feminine traits or values or qualities. Then look at the Gospel—or look at any of the great Church documents—and you'll find a very feminine spirituality.

It's a spirituality of compassion, suffering, love, self-sacrifice. Everything they say a woman should be about is what they say the Church and the Gospel should be about. Docility to the will of God, a sense of service to others, total commitment to the will of God— it's all there. It's very feminine—it's just not permitted for females to participate in it fully.

Q: How did you come to that understanding?

A: It will come as a great surprise to you. I think I've probably known it, as maybe anybody knows it, down deep. But I came to an articulated position on it after the Roman Catholic bishops wrote their peace pastoral, "The Challenge of Peace."

Somebody asked me to do a feminist analysis of the peace pastoral. I decided I'd take the basic psychological categories of the feminine paradigm and see to what degree these qualities exist in the peace pastoral.

I said to myself, "Joan, don't do this. You will be so depressed if you find just one more male document among all those written by all of the males of the world." But I did it, and out of seven categories, five were clearly feminine.

The only place it isn't feminine by that criteria is that the bishops aren't asking for unilateral disarmament, which would have been a very feminine thing to do. To just say, "Well, I'm not going to be a part of this. This is wrong, and so I'm not going to be a part of this. This is wrong, and so I'm not going to do it . . . . Uncle." Because women know how to lose. They're used to losing with such grace.

So, my last paragraph was more of a prayer than it was a generalizing device. I said, "And here is this very feminine document. How amazing. And it is one of the most powerful documents that the bishops have written. How amazing, how wonderful, how strange."

And then I began to think, the Gospel carries these same qualities, and the great social encyclicals carry these same qualities. And so here we have, as I see it, a Church and a Gospel with a high degree of feminine spirituality, denying females full inclusion and immersion in it.

Working my way through that analysis and looking back, I know I fit in the faith. Are the male overlay of structure, and the male overlay of language, and the male overlay of authority, and the male overlay of process difficult, smothering sometimes, impossible often? Yes! But the structures and the authority models and the processes and the visible control aren't the spirituality, they're the institution.

So I hear the Gospels. My feminine heart hears a deep, deep cry to my feminine self.

I always think that the chapter in the Benedictine Rule that is being lost to this period in history is chapter seven on humility. I see the Benedictine Rule as a very feminine thing.

It is calling men in the Roman Empire, men in any empire, men in any culture or century, who are trained from the cradle to be highly independent, highly individualistic, and highly self-seeking, to live in community. To live for the other. To pour themselves out without any reward. That's a very feminine thing.

And Benedict of Nursia doesn't permit rank or status in the community. He wants a community of equals. Here is a person saying pour yourself out, give yourself away, trust the stranger, make yourself vulnerable—very feminine.

Vulnerability is not something most males think they aspire to. They're to be protectors. They're to be the ultimate strength. They're there to be on top of things.

Obedience is only a masculine ideal when it serves the macho system. But a man is trained to get on top to be the one to give the orders. A woman is trained to listen, to hear, to be docile. The Rule says listen and hear and be docile.

And then there's this capstone chapter on humility. Humility! In the Roman Empire! Are you kidding? From the sons of nobles?—who are the people comprising these communities. Humility is a very feminine thing.

So all my life I have felt comfortable in the faith. I have never felt that I was being wrenched into something that was contrary to me. But I wonder if both the Gospel and the Rule of Benedict aren't the strong countersign that they are because they are calling me away from the male values of every other institution. And is that why you don't have as many men comfortable either with monasteries or with the Gospel?

And who are your holy men? They just don't fit the image of the field commander. They're very gentle. They're the local monk, they're St. Francis of Assisi, and they're Jesus Christ—all very gentle figures.

So here we have a Gospel that's built, and a tradition that's built, on tremendous vulnerability, self-sacrifice, service to the other, love, and compassion, in a culture that is telling men that the real man is exactly the opposite. So inside my heart, I'm at home. Inside the structures, I'm not.

Q: It's obvious that those kinds of concepts are questioned in the Church. Why is that understanding so threatening to the structures?

A: I think that the people who are threatened by that are very sincerely concerned about what would happen to a church that doesn't have a very well-developed, hierarchical authority pattern. They fear the erosion of the deposit of faith. And they always talk about it as if there would be no recognized authority in the Scriptures or in the Church. I would simply argue that that authority wouldn't be eroded; it would be strengthened, because it would be shared.

This is not a question of whether or not church members accept authority. Of course they do. What is being questioned is whether or not the full revelation of the Gospel can possibly be worked out in the structures in which we're attempting to live it.

Q: You mentioned earlier the male overlay of language as one of the problems. Can you say more about that issue and how wo-

men's understanding of spirituality is changing our understanding of God and our use of language?

A: My professional background is in social psychology and communication theory. Ten years ago I wrote my first article on that
subject and called it "Brotherly Love in the Roman Catholic
Church." What I tried to point out in that article is the notion that
language structures thought.

The basic principle is that what is not in the language is not in
the mind. So if you are ignoring women in Church language, or
lumping women under a so-called generic term which is only
generic half of the time, then what you have done is erase half the
population of the earth. They can exist only when somebody else
calls them into existence. So half of us are left to figure out when
they mean us and when they don't.

That's why in the Hebrew tradition the idea of naming, of giving
identity to, is a very important part of the theology. And we recognize it at that level. But we have failed to recognize it when we say,
"Dearly beloved brethren, let us pray for the grace to recognize that
we are all sons of God."

I never got that grace—that's how I'm sure that kind of interces-
sion doesn't work. I remember from the time I was five years old,
looking around the church, knowing that they had forgotten somebody; they'd forgotten me, and I was in the church. I was not a son
of God. I was a daughter of God and very comfortable with that.

The whole notion that the language comes out of a woman's
envy of men is ridiculous! It comes out of a woman's recognition of
the greatness of the creation of womanhood. If God could afford to
make us separately, then it seems somebody could talk to us
separately.

As I read the tale, God addressed Adam and Eve separately.
God didn't call up Abraham and say, "I just presume Sarah will get
her part of the message." Throughout creation history there has
been direct confirmation of the fact that God and a woman can have
direct conversation and contact. We've lost that in our languages;
and then we act as if it's not important.

Linguists can tell from a language what is important to a people. They may find archaeological elements they cannot account for in the language. They'll know that those elements were not important to the culture, and the people's way of thinking subsumed multiple things under other categories.

The Eskimos have 18 separate words for snow, because snow is central in Eskimo life. Americans have at least that many words for car. We call it hatchback and Taurus and Ford, Diplomat and Regal and Oldsmobile and Chevy. The language for car in this country is almost unlimited. But when you ask for two pronouns for the human race, they tell you you're going too far! The only thing that a woman can conclude is that she is not as important as the multiple kinds of cars, and wood, and fishing poles in the world—let alone guns.

When you look at that from a broader theological construct, you begin to look at language about God. You cannot understand the problem about God language unless you are willing to realize that it is not that we are just discovering a feminine dimension of God; it is that the recognition of the feminine dimension of God, a cosmic dimension of God, has been suppressed. It isn't that we shouldn't call God "Father." It is that we shouldn't call God only Father. It isn't that Jesus wasn't male. It is that Jesus was a great deal more than male.

The oldest, most basic, most traditional theologies I know do not claim that Jesus came to become male. Jesus came to be flesh. And when you subsume all of theological language, all God talk, in male terms, then you have lost a sense not only of who and what woman is, but of who and what God is.

We are in a state of great linguistic, and therefore great theological, paucity. We have reduced God to one of the tiniest elements of creation. And we say that's everything God is. That is heresy raised to a fine art.

The new calf in the desert is maleness. While Moses ascends to do dialogue with the transcendent spiritual God, the people in the desert below turn God into a golden calf. And while we claim great spiritual insight and full revelation in the churches, and sophisticated understanding for our creative God, we have turned God into a male.

The Scriptures don't do that. The oldest litanies of the Church don't do it. Right up until the last century, God was multiple images. God was rock, God was mother, God was hen, God was Creator, God was mighty, God was love, God was all the divine praises.

I can remember having to stretch my little mind when we said great litanies in the Catholic school. I can remember being a third grader just unable to take in this God. I knew God was ineffable. Because when Sister prayed with us, she told us God was all these things.

Now if you dare to assume that "Sophia Wisdom," the feminine side of God, is still with us, you touch the raw edge of an insecure male church. And that's a shame; it's a great disservice to God.

Prior to the Babylonian captivity, we see many more images for God in Scripture than we do afterward because apparently—and this is speculation by some of the historians—there was a great concern not to have Judaism confused with the pagan ritual and worship of the Canaanites.

Nevertheless, the notion of wisdom in the Scripture was clearly recognized as the feminine side of God. In Proverbs, wisdom is always a female figure. For example, from Proverbs 4: "Get wisdom, get understanding, do not forget or turn aside from the word I utter. Forsake her not, and she will preserve you. Love her, and she will safeguard you. Get wisdom at the cost of all you have. Get understanding, extol her and she will exalt you. She will bring you honors if you will embrace her."

Isaiah also uses feminine references for God. Jeremiah uses feminine references. Jesus uses feminine references. And the Church in its early litanies used cosmic references, or non-gendered references, always.

It's in our own time, in the attempt to keep women in their place, to make sure that the full creation does not break out in a woman, that language is used to keep reminding her that she is not as normative of God as a man is—because God is father, therefore God is male, therefore males are closer to God. Language is a key function in bringing women to the fullness of creation.

Q: What is happening to women as they're rediscovering their closeness to God and the part of God within them, and as the language and women's understanding of their place in the Church are changing?

A: I think a great new sense of grace is coming into women. I know people want to attach a secular language to it—that it is aggressive, or at least assertive, or it is uppity or out of line. But I think it's what happens to a person who comes face-to-face with the grace of God in life.

I think it's what happened to Mary, the mother of God. I think you become capable of anything. And no system, no matter how sincere, can ever again convince you that your relationship to God must be mediated by a man, or that God doesn't want to deal directly with you. Or that God certainly doesn't want you to have the fullness of grace. Somehow you begin to know that what is going on inside you is of God. It's both a center and channel of grace. And that's extremely important.

Q: And with that happening to women, there's also a wholeness that's coming to the Church that hasn't been there in a long time.

A: I really believe that. I haven't seen anything yet that walks well on one leg. And I honestly believe that we're going to be a truer Church when we recognize in one another, in every other, the call of God to total fullness.

It just has to happen, because we complement one another. But you and I complement one another as much as you and any male minister complement one another. We are all small pieces of the mind and face of God. And as long as we are erasing half of us, we're never going to get a full picture of God.

Part III

The Balance of Time:
Spirituality to Sustain a Life of Ministry

Q: You said earlier that contemplation sometimes means binding up the wounded person along the road. Would you say more about what you mean by that?

A: If the contemplative life has to bring us to an awareness of the presence of God and a consciousness of the mandates of Jesus, how else can you purport to live a contemplative life? Contemplation is not an excursion into the "airy fairy."

Contemplation is an immersion into the mind of God and the life of Christ to such an extent that the way you live your own life can never again be quite the same. That's why people change. Because they're drawing from a different set of values and a different goal.

The goal is the building up of the kingdom where the widows are cared for, orphans are loved, the measures are equal, dreaming is possible, and everybody is brought to fullness of life. If you're living the contemplative life, then eventually you have to come face-to-face with your obligation to be touched by all those dimensions.

That's why Thomas Merton had the most contemporary prayer life in the world. That's why you ought to be able to go to any enclosed monastery and get good counsel about your own life and the circumstances of the world you're living in.

There's a historian who said that the monastery confronts the castle with a question mark. The values that are derived from the contemplative life are the filter through which the contemplative sees the world. And they are consequently the critique that the contemplative brings to the constructs and institutions of a society. These values should never be "other than" or "out of" the world. The world should be seen through those values. And the contemplative speaks of the incongruity of those values.

As a result, you have to be part of the binding up of the wounds of the world. And you can do it in many, many ways. You can do it by critiquing the world, if you live in an enclosed community. You can do it by restructuring the world, if you live in an active community or a monastic community. You can do it by providing alternative models for the world. You can do it by working within the world. How you do it doesn't matter, but you must do it. It cannot not be done.

Q: You entered this community when it was more enclosed, and all the sisters were involved in a similar type of ministry. Some years ago renewal happened, and women expanded their understanding of ministry. And now you are all involved in different types of things. How has that new understanding of ministry affected your own understanding of spirituality?

A: The community I entered in 1952 was semicloistered, which meant that ministry was brought to you, you didn't really go to it. It's not so much the spirituality that's changed but the demonstration of ministries that has changed. In the mid-19th century in Germany, the German government passed a law that said it would no longer provide pension monies or support monies for religious communities that did not provide a service to the state. In other words, there were to be no parasites. That's a very good law.

Monasteries in their ancient forms had never been parasites. On the contrary, monasteries had been the center and the structure of public activities. It's not a myth that Benedictine, Cistercian, and Trappist communities became centers of order and development when the Roman Empire fell.

When Roman legions and Roman legates no longer existed to coordinate activities or to provide services, the monasteries were the only places giving direction to the people. Monasteries either deliberately moved into a territory in order to provide that kind of service, or the people eventually settled around the monastery.

And the monasteries owned large farms. They were very important in the agricultural development of Europe, and they began to employ people. The abbot became the lord mayor of the village that grew up around a monastery. To this day, in small villages in Europe, the center and central institution is often a monastery.

It's important to remember that at a point in the early Middle Ages, the government and the Church were the same body. It was a king who wanted Benedictine monasteries to be every place, because he knew that would be good for the empire.

Now in the High Middle Ages, after the economy became urban and commercial, and the poor became more of a roaming band than a landed band, religious communities began to minister to the poor differently. Monastic communities, however, stayed on the land where they were, and were inclined to become more and more self-sufficient and self-contained than they had been in the preceding period in history.

It's out of that cultural and historical background that the German government said that it was not going to give state pension monies to groups that were not performing a service for the state. At that point a number of monasteries, particularly Benedictine monasteries, opened schools. Again, schools had been very popular and very common demonstrations of Benedictine ministry until the rise of the university system and the development of both a public and an independent private educational system.

My own community's history started in the mid-19th century. You had the newly-developing concept that the monastery is to provide a service to the people of the area which was obviously not going to be agricultural any more. As a result, monasteries of women who had the concept of cloister imposed on them around the 13th century, as a protective device as well as an ascetical device, were then somewhat welcomed back into the ministerial mainstream.

So my community was simply a reflection of 19th century monasticism in the German setting. We were semicloistered, which means that people do come in for services, but the sisters do not normally go to other places.

We had an entire mission system developed. By 1875 they had developed the notion that everyone didn't have to come into the major monastery. Groups of five to 20 sisters would go a hundred miles away from the mother house in Erie, Pennsylvania, and they would begin a little monastery, not independent of this one. The prioress of this monastery was their prioress, but the life was duplicated. They would live on the school property, and the children would be brought to them. They were still keeping this new model of cloistered life that was civic and ecclesiastical in a new way, with a new intent.

Now there are two important dimensions of that response: The community stays monastic throughout, and it gives service throughout. So when Vatican II issued the call to renewal, renewal of ministry was as legitimate a subject as renewal of prayer life, renewal of community life, renewal of personal life, and we began to look at how to stay monastic and do service.

Out of that review came the notion that you didn't simply have to teach, that other kinds of service are needed. And perhaps Benedictines don't become Benedictines to become teachers, they become Benedictines to become Benedictines. What we're about now is doing ministry, providing necessary service, in line with a Benedictine vocation which is communal in its expression and its spirituality. The point is that the structures have changed, the spirituality has not.

Q: Your community made a decision to embrace peacemaking as a vocation. How does that fit with your own tradition, spirituality and understanding?

A: That is a really important development of your last question. At one time our ministries obviously had become highly institutional. When this review of 20th-century ministry began to develop, we discovered that there were multiple gifts in the community that matched multiple needs in this locale. We began to pursue them and to enable them to develop. And as a result of the study of Benedictinism and monastic spirituality, we began to ask ourselves what ministry or ministries are most appropriate to a Benedictine charism?

The one continuing thread from earliest time until now in the Benedictine tradition is the tradition of peacemaking. We know historically that early Christians did not participate in the military. And though historians struggle with whether the major concern was that they could not participate in the emperor worship common to soldiers in the Roman Empire or whether the primary concern was that Christians do not kill, the fact remains that the data reflects unquestionably that the early Christians simply believed "Love one another" and "Thou shalt not kill" were absolute mandates.

Now at the time of Marcus Aurelius, in the 2nd century, and then again with the legitimization of Christianity by Constantine in the 4th century, many Christians were not schooled in that history, and so a lot of Christian soldiers were soldiering. There was one military law in the Roman Empire. Conscription was not a law of the empire. Mercenaries fought most of the wars. But the one law that did exist was that the son of a Roman officer was required to become a soldier.

Martin of Tours' father was a general in the Roman legions, but his son showed no disposition to that whatsoever. He indicated to his father that he believed that soldiering was not acceptable for a Christian. And so the boy was kidnapped at his father's own direction when he was 15 or 16 and taken off to the barracks to be trained as a soldier.

But the more he was trained, the more reluctant he became. Until finally, the records show, when he was ordered to the front he simply took off his sword and presented it to the Roman commander. When they accused him of being cowardly, his answer was, "I am no coward. I do not do this out of fear, I do this out of faith. And to prove my point, tomorrow you may send me to the front, but I will go without my sword." So they let this boy leave the legions.

For a while he demonstrated his opposition to this use of Christians or to this practice by Christians, and eventually he started a religious community. Now, monks were recognized as pacifists. You simply couldn't commandeer a monk into military service, and everyone knew it.

That pacifist tradition is still honored by governments. We don't draft monks, priests, or clerics, because we recognize that from time immemorial this is a peacemaking tradition. In the Middle Ages, monks were the first groups to raise the notion of rules for modern warfare. It's the monks who first attempted to promote the peace of God, and then to promote the compromised position of the truce of God which says: If you must fight, then all we ask for is an agreement that you don't fight on Thursday, because Thursday is the memorial of the Ascension, and you don't fight on Friday, because Friday is the memorial of the Passion, and you don't fight on Saturday, because Saturday is the memorial of the Entombment, and, of course, you can't fight on Sunday, because Sunday is the memorial of the Resurrection.

It was medieval monasteries and monks who tried to control this open season on human beings. It was the medieval monks who did a great deal to develop the whole notion of chivalry. If you are going to be a soldier, there is even a way to be a Christian soldier. And during this period, a lot of the writings on this topic came out of the monasteries.

Now if you're Benedictine and the most ancient motto of the order is "Pax," and you live in the 20th century where you are now capable of replicating 1,600,000 Hiroshimas, then surely there is some special obligation on the part of the Benedictine to address that continuing issue.

That first chapter of this ancient rule says, "Listen to the precepts of the Master, incline the ear of your heart, and cheerfully receive and faithfully execute the admonitions of your loving Father, that by the toil of obedience you may return to him from whom by the sloth of disobedience you have gone away. To you, therefore, my speech is now directed, who, giving up your own will, take up the strong and most excellent arms of obedience to do battle for Christ the Lord, the true King." It's a military metaphor used to indicate that the *militia Christi*, the soldier of Christ, doesn't fight the way everybody else fights. And that if you are of Christ, your soldiering is different. Given that kind of history and that awareness of the continuation of an institutionalized pacifist tradition, and a moment in history when the shift was from an institutional ministry to multiple ministries done in the name of the community, we had to deal with the question, "What ministry are you able to do in the community that you would not be able to do as well alone? What is the community ministry?"

For us, that community ministry was hospitality. That community ministry was community. That community ministry was prayer—to be a place of prayer for other people to be able to dip into and out of as they needed. But it was also a ministry of peace. We decided that what we needed in this day and age was not a particular service that we gave through institutions that we developed, but a corporate commitment to a policy to which we would all give witness, no matter what individual ministry we are engaged in at that time.

Out of that comes our corporate commitment in this community to nuclear disarmament, and especially the relationship of sexism to militarism. We simply educate ourselves consistently and regularly about the effects of militarism in this country, and particularly the effects on women of machismo as a distortion of the culture and of relationships. And wherever we are, we make every attempt to bring that agenda to consciousness in that place.

For example, a second grade teacher may develop a whole project on peace cranes so that second graders in the United States send the great Japanese symbol of peace to second graders in Japan. Our nurses work at developing a consciousness in the medical community about the effects of radiation and what the medical establishment would be able to do in response. Our peace and justice center, frankly, preceded our community definition of the corporate commitment, but was our earliest and most obvious community answer to this relationship of the Benedictine tradition to the pacifist tradition. All of those things just came together then for all of us.

Q: I have the sense that your community's prayer life and ministry life are very integrated, and that they grow out of each other. I often hear people who describe themselves as Christian activists ask, "Where do I find time for my prayer life, or how do I integrate prayer into ministry, or how do I find balance in my life?" Could you address that?

A: I certainly can, because if there's any question that we go through regularly, it is that one. In the first place, I can tell you that after years of experience of community living, and with all the change that came with renewal, and all the major issues that we are grappling with in this world, you do not find time for prayer. Nobody finds time for prayer. You either take time for it or you don't get it. If I am waiting for it to be given to me, it shall never be given.

I think if I reach that point, I have begun the last trek down a very short road. Because the fuel runs out. The energy goes down.

I become my own enemy. I can no longer remember why I ever decided to do this. And if I can't remember why I decided to do it, I can't figure out how I can go on with it. Because I'm tired and the vision just gets dimmer and dimmer.

On days when I have worn myself out most in behalf of peacemaking and women, I have gone to bed knowing that when I get up the next day, we will still be a militaristic society, and sexism will still reign. So if I take an additional 30 minutes a day away from the problem, not only will the problem still be there, but I will probably be able to spend the next day on it which I couldn't have done otherwise.

The balance problem depends on what you call balance. The worst thing that ever happened to balance is the light bulb. When the light bulb was invented, all of us got a balance problem. You've got it if you're the local pacifist, you've got it if you're the local bishop, you've got it if you're the local store clerk. There used to be a time when you had to quit because the sun went down. And there's not much you can do with tallow candles that will shake the ankles of the world.

We have turned night into eternal day. And most people don't even realize that we never allow night to come. We just keep pushing back the confines of night. So balance was once built into us circadian creatures by some very natural process. We have managed to defeat nature and it is defeating us.

Balance, then, is no longer necessarily daily, or even necessarily cyclical, unless I make it cyclical. Therefore, I have to have great appreciation for the concept of Sabbath, of holy leisure, of taking time for rest and reflection, so that my activity time has more quality.

I'm sure everybody in the world who doesn't know me has some terribly clear picture of Joan Chittister as high-level activist. Wrong. I can't get anywhere at all unless at about 8 o'clock every single normal night of my life I'm in my room reading for two-and-a-half to three hours. And by normal I mean the three or four nights a week that I'm not traveling or speaking or involved in community events. Or I may spend those nights just being. I am capable of being. That inserts balance into my life.

I don't have to run from 6 a.m. to midnight every day and fall into my bed just long enough to get up and run again. There is a necessary cycle of reflection and integration that provides energy for the rest of life. I had a spiritual director who used to say, "The empty vessel must be filled." And those of us who think we can go on forever pouring ourselves out without at the same time filling ourselves up need to read the seventh chapter of Benedict on the rule of humility. The first degree of humility is to allow God to be God. And we're just not going to be able to do it without becoming a more contemplative part of this ongoing cycle of development.

So, what does all that mean? It means that prayer, in my opinion, is absolutely essential both to consciousness and to serenity. And that our important work will be done with more impact and import if we bring to it our best selves. And our best selves come when we are calling ourselves to conversion in the Scriptures, and constantly putting on the mind of Christ. Balance is something we have to achieve for the sake of the long haul.

Q: You're talking about prayer mostly in terms of nurturing ourselves. You made a comment earlier that our prayer isn't about changing the mind of God. But we are people who are very connected to the world's suffering and believe in a God who hears the cries of the poor and those who clamor for justice. And we believe that God hears our cries for justice as well. We offer petitions and intercessions. Can you talk about that kind of prayer in relationship to our ministry, in relationship to the suffering we see?

A: The Scripture tells us very clearly that God hears the cry of the poor. And God notes it and records it and watches. And on the basis of that hearing, God will someday judge what we did with the cries we heard.

Prayer asks for the strength to respond, for the insight to know, for the grace to do, and for the courage to endure. And I believe God gives us all these things. When we become conscious of those needs, we have the promise, "Ask and you shall receive," and the assurance of God's presence with us.

We're not talking to the great cornucopia God. If that were our theology, we would soon have to begin to doubt our God. The grace has come, the strength has come, the awareness has come, the courage has come, the repentance has come, both for us who are rich and for the poor who know that their ultimate salvation is in God. In the meantime, you and I are praying for the grace to get through our own smallness so that we too can hear the cry of the poor, and change our own lives accordingly, because God is hearing and God will judge on the basis of those cries.

Q: I think many of us who are active in ministry and in touch with people's suffering find it easy to offer petitions and difficult to offer praise. We have so many visions for change that it's difficult to see what we have and be thankful.

A: That comment is related to our previous discussion on the place of joy in the Christian community and the notion of recognizing the signs of hope. Hope is a phenomenal Christian virtue. And not to be able to praise is not to be able to hope.

That's one of the ways in which the poor evangelize us to such a depth, because in many instances they're not complaining about the things we're complaining about for them. They know what the necessities of life really are. They know when they have them, and they know how demanding of praise those things become.

So if we lose sight of praise, either we are not seeing the presence of God in our world, we have failed to note the distinction between needs and wants, or we are on the brink of thinking that only what we call good is what God calls good. Or we've lost a sense of time. We want everything in our time instead of in the fullness of time.

Scripture says that the great good—Jesus—only came in the fullness of time. We don't know when the fullness of time is for anything. We must live in praise that we've done what we can to contribute to the coming of the fullness of time.

So, should there be intercessory prayer? You bet. And does God wait to hear or respond to the needs? Yes. And are we both breaking open ourselves and the consciousness of the cosmic in intercessory prayer? Of course. But we are also recognizing in praise that we've received a lot of things that we never thought to pray for, because God is God and loves us and continually builds up our hope in the fullness of time by the things we weren't even smart enough, holy enough, to recognize that we needed.

That's my theology in a nutshell. Of course, we cry out to God with what we believe are our needs, knowing that God will always respond to our needs. But the question is, what do we really need?

The purpose of that is not to rationalize suffering. And it is not intended to deter us from dealing with suffering on the human level. On the contrary, we deal out of our concern for the fullness of the kingdom, knowing that the fullness will come in God's good time.